A
Common
Core

The InterAct Series

GEORGE W. RENWICK, Series Editor

A *Common* *Core*

THAIS AND AMERICANS

JOHN PAUL FIEG

REVISED BY
ELIZABETH MORTLOCK

INTERCULTURAL PRESS, INC.

Library of Congress Cataloging-in-Publication Data

Fieg, John P., 1941–
    Thais and North Americans: interact 3/John Paul Fieg, author; revised by Elizabeth Mortlock.
        p.   cm.
    Bibliography: p.
    ISBN 0-933662-80-7
    1. National characteristics, Thai. 2. National charac-
teristics, American. 3. Intercultural communication.
4. Work ethic—Thailand. 5. Work ethic—United States.
6. Business etiquette—Thailand. 7. Business etiquette—
United States. 8. Thailand—Civilization. 9. United
States—Civilization—1970–   I. Mortlock, Elizabeth.
II. Title.
DS569.F544   1989   89-2124
303.48′2593073—dc20   CIP

Printed in the United States of America.

Contents

Preface

This was one of the first books in a series—the *Interact Series*—which explains the interaction between Americans and people from other countries and cultures. It is with some pleasure, therefore, that we publish this revision of John Fieg's fine work.

A cultural interaction study like this one probes, explains and predicts what happens when individuals who have grown up in contrasting cultures meet, eat, joke, argue, negotiate and cooperate with one another. Such a study makes clear what each person must do in order to become a clever competitor or a trusted colleague and friend.

This volume and other volumes in the *Interact Series* explain how people from one culture see those in another, what exactly they expect from each other, how they affect each other when they are together, and how what is said and done by one embarrasses, frustrates, motivates, impresses or angers the other.

John Fieg, who wrote the first version of *A Common Core,* is uniquely qualified to explore Thai and American cultures and how the people from each relate with each other. He is also a very capable writer who can convey his understanding of both groups in an engaging manner. John grew up in midwestern United States, completed his undergraduate studies at the University of Notre

Dame and a master's degree in journalism at Northwestern University. He first lived in Thailand as a Peace Corps volunteer. After returning to the U.S. to obtain a law degree at George Washington University and to work at the Washington International Center and the East-West Center in Hawaii, he returned to Thailand where he was an English specialist at Sukhothai Thammathirat University for four years. John is currently back in Hawaii, teaching at Pacific International Language School and writing textbooks for English as a Second Language.

It was fortunate that Elizabeth Mortlock was available to revise the original version of *A Common Core*. Liz is a professional writer who has lived in Hong Kong, Singapore, Jakarta and Bangkok and is currently living in São Paulo, Brazil. The end of her stay in Thailand, where she lived for four years, coincided with the completion of this revision. While in Bangkok, she worked as a freelance writer for the United States Information Service, the United States Agency for International Development, the *Bangkok Post*, the Asia Foundation and *Living* magazine. For a brief period each summer, Liz and her husband, David, and their two children can be found in Camden, Maine.

We are confident that the readers of *A Common Core* will find it a helpful resource in understanding the contrasts and similarities of Thai and U.S. cultures, will more thoroughly enjoy associating with people from the other culture, and will work more productively with them.

George W. Renwick
Editor, *Interact Series*.

Acknowledgments
Revised Edition

This new edition of the *Thai InterAct* has been revised and updated to reflect economic, social, and political developments in Thailand during the past decade and, in particular, the change and evolution which has occurred in the Thai business community in Bangkok as more and more Thais gain experience with Western and international business practices. Much valuable information was gained from a study undertaken in 1986 by the revisions editor and Mayuri Sukwiwat (who contributed substantially to the first edition of this book), with financing from the United States Information Service in Bangkok. For this study, over one hundred Thais and Americans, both in Thailand and in the United States, were interviewed and polled on Thai-American cultural differences. For this revision the revisions editor conducted further interviews with Thai and American members of the academic and business communities in Bangkok. In addition to those who contributed their observations but prefer to remain anonymous, special thanks go to Allen Choate of The Asia Foundation, Virginia Di Crocco of Chulalongkorn University, James V. Di Crocco,

Michael Fonner of Mahidol University, Patchanee Sutheevita-
nunt of Citibank, and Roy Weiland of Esso and the American
Chamber of Commerce.

Elizabeth Mortlock
Bangkok
April 1988

Acknowledgments
First Edition

In writing this study I have tried to draw on and synthesize
materials from several sources—from books and articles available
in libraries, from a short questionnaire that was sent to a few Thais
who have worked with Americans, and from personal interviews.
During the course of the study a number of people were kind
enough to share their thoughts and considerable experience with
me. I would here like to thank them all for their many perceptive
comments and for their extraordinary patience in answering my
persistent questions.

Three graduate students at the University of Hawaii, Peansiri
Ekniyom Vongvipanond, Thamrong Chomaitong, and Kannikar
Chomaitong, made many helpful comparisons between Thais and
Americans generally. Pana Thongmeearkorm, an East-West Center
grantee and a professor at Chulalonghorn University, skillfully
analyzed different business procedures; and another East-West
Center grantee, Monthatip Krishnamura, provided the perspec-
tive of a communications specialist.

Several members of the Thai business community in Hawaii
interrupted their busy schedules to compare their experiences in
the U.S. and Thailand. Somsak Rungsongsinthu spoke from be-

xii

hind the counter of his Waikiki jewelry store. Chaiyong Vithay-
awongruchi and Boonmee Prasertpenkul supplied the insights of
recent business administration graduates who are now putting
their schooling to work in the competitive restaurant field. (They
also served an excellent lunch!) Wilaipahn Wongvanij, holder of
a master's degree in anthropology and now manager of the Asian-
Thai Trade Center, was particularly perceptive in relating business
practices to cultural values.

Three faculty members at the University of Hawaii—Segei
Naya (economics), Jack Bilmes (anthropology), and Pongsuwan
Bilmes (Thai language)—brought the perspectives of their respective disciplines to bear on Thai/American values, and the latter
threw considerable light on relevant episodes in Thai history. Two
other professors who were in Hawaii for the summer, Brian Foster
of the State University of New York at Binghamton and Gordon
Redding of the University of Hong Kong, kindly shared their
expertise and materials. Sriprinya Ramakomut, professor of business administration at Howard University and also at the National
Institute for Development Administration in Thailand, was especially helpful in discussing interaction between Thai and American businessmen.

Thanks are also in order to Bronwen Solyom of the University
of Hawaii library staff, who kindly provided me a carrel in Hamil-
ton Library, and to my sister and brother-in-law, Mary Ann and
John Boyd, who had the unenviable task of searching out some old
materials that I had abandoned in Illinois and sending them on to
me in Hawaii.

Finally, I would like to particularly thank Mayuri Sukwiwat, a
visiting researcher at the Cultural Learning Institute at the East-
West Center. Not only did she graciously share her time and
insights, but she also helped locate interviewees, supplied me with
several books, and arranged for the questionnaire to be distributed
in Bangkok. Her help throughout all stages of this study has been
indispensable.

What follows, then, will reflect library research, answers to a
questionnaire, and comments from the interviewees, but the

ultimate responsibility for the content is of course my own. I hope that this study will play some small part in furthering mutual understanding and respect. I also hope that it is *sanùke!*

John Paul Fieg
September 1978

About Romanized
Thai Words and Tones

In this book, Thai words are spelled in Romanized script. The Thai language is normally written in Thai script, but since few non-Thais can read Thai script, words are sometimes spelled out in Roman characters which closely reflect the Thai sounds. For example, the glossy Thai International Airline magazine is called *Sawasdee* (meaning "hello"). If it were written in Thai characters, the name would be totally illegible to non-Thai passengers, so it is spelled out in Roman characters.

Aside from the different characters used, another major difference between Thai and English is the use of tones. Many Thai words change their meaning according to the tone used. There are five possible tones in Thai: ´ high tone, ∧ falling tone, middle tone (no tone mark), ∨ rising tone, and ` low tone. In English, for example, the word *dog* means only one thing whether you say it in a high or low tone. The Thai word *ma*, in contrast, has three meanings depending on the tone used: *má* (high tone, means "horse"), *ma* (middle tone, means "come"), and *mà* (low tone, means "dog").

To enable readers to pronounce the Romanized Thai words accurately, tone marks are indicated. In monosyllabic words, only one tone is used. In multisyllabic words, the tone may change with each syllable, as in the word *Mekong*, the name of a river and of a popular brand of Thai whiskey, which is pronounced *Mê* (falling tone) *kǒng* (rising tone).

LAOS

VIETNAM

Lampang

Udon Thani

BURMA

THAILAND

Ubon Ratchathanı

Nakhon Sawan

Nakhon Ratchasima

Bangkok

KAMPUCHEA
(CAMBODIA)

Gulf of Thailand

VIETNAM

Nakhon Si
Thammarat

Malay
Peninsula

Songkhla

MALAYSIA

1

Introduction

For more than 150 years, Thais and Americans have been developing cultural, economic and political relationships. As early as 1821 the first American ship reached Thailand. In 1833 the first Thai-American treaty, the Treaty of Amity and Commerce, was signed in Bangkok. During the 1850s and 1860s Thailand's King Mongkut exchanged correspondence with three American presidents—Pierce, Buchanan, and Lincoln.

During World War II members of the Free Thai movement joined Americans in resisting the Japanese; and during the Vietnam War the U.S. and Thailand supported one another in protecting regional security against Communist forces. In the past thirty years the U.S. has made more than $800 million (in grants and loans) available to Thailand for support in the spheres of education, health, and security, as well as for social, economic, and political development. The U.S. government has provided funding for some twelve thousand Thai students to study in the United States.

Today, with Thailand's substantial economic development, the two countries have become important trading partners, and the level of U.S. foreign aid to Thailand has dropped considerably. American multinationals such as Citibank, Esso (as Exxon is still known in Thailand), and IBM have large offices in Thailand. The

1

U.S. is Thailand's biggest export market. More than eight thousand Thais study in U.S. institutions each year, many in the field of business. Nancy Reagan's visit to Thailand in 1986 highlighted Thai-U.S. joint efforts to combat the international narcotics problem. Thousands of Thais live and work in the U.S., with a large concentration in the Los Angeles area; and thousands of Americans live and work in Thailand as business people, U.S. government and embassy officials, technical consultants, university professors, Peace Corps volunteers, missionaries, etc.—many, of course, with their families. Tourists in large numbers from both countries gawk at each other's famous sites.

In recent decades Thais and Americans have learned a great deal about each other's cultures, though it could be argued that Thais know considerably more about the U.S. than Americans know about Thailand. As they live and work more closely together, both need to become increasingly perceptive and understanding about their similarities and differences. The purpose of this book is to shed light on these similarities and differences so that each can have a clearer understanding of the other's ways of thinking and doing things. Only when both have insights of this sort will they be able to pursue effectively the kinds of harmonious social and business interactions required for success in dealing with each other.

In order to cast light on the two cultures, it will obviously be necessary to generalize if any type of meaningful comparison is to be made. Yet, because both Thais and Americans have a tendency to think of themselves as unique individuals, they might resist the notion that there is such a thing as an "average" American or "typical" Thai. If one probes deeply enough, however, it does appear that the peoples of any country do possess certain basic assumptions or values which will generally manifest themselves in their opinions and behavior.

This, of course, does not mean that every American or every Thai is going to act in accordance with a generalized cultural value at all times—or even that the same individual will act according to the same value at all times. What it does mean is that a tendency or trend can be discerned so that a country or culture can be said to be more individualistic or group-centered, more hierarchical or egalitarian, more practical or more philosophical, etc. Seen in this light—as tendencies rather than absolute precepts—cultural values do help in explaining patterns of thought or behavior which would otherwise be inscrutable to someone raised in a different cultural environment.

There is one further problem. Given the cultural and geographical diversity within the United States and the varied web of ethnic backgrounds from which Americans come, it could be argued that a New York WASP yuppie, a Chicago rabbi, a Kansas farmer, a Vietnamese-American high school valedictorian, and a Mexican-American dentist have few cultural similarities. How can we say that there is any one American pattern?

Despite the pride many cultural groups hold in their own cultural heritage, waves of immigrants to the United States have found their sons and daughters adopting American cultural characteristics which play themselves out in such things as the use of the English language, the free enterprise system, the judicial system, compulsory education, representative government, and mass popular culture.

Many Americans—including those from ethnic minorities— have suddenly realized their distinct "Americanness" after being abroad for only a brief time. Suddenly immersed in a different culture, they recognize how much they share in basic values, attitudes, and behaviors with other Americans. The differences that had seemed so pronounced in the past become muted as they sense a previously unrecognized similarity and see the much greater differences between them and their host culture.

In generalizing about Thai values, an analogous—though not identical—problem appears, for Thais live in two very different worlds—the world of Bangkok and the world of the village. The gulf between the two can be measured not only in miles but also in centuries. The vast majority of the population live in small villages and cultivate rice and other agricultural products. The heads of the families in the rural areas rarely have more than a primary education. In small villages few farm families have electricity or running water. Consumer needs are met by small general stores which carry such items as flour, sugar, cigarettes, kitchen utensils, hats, shoes, soap, flashlights, rope, nails, and buffalo bells.

Bangkok, by contrast, is a sprawling, modern metropolis. Department stores carry an incredible variety of modern consumer goods. Restaurants serve food from every corner of the globe, and the level of education of the average resident far outstrips his rural counterpart. Because so many Bangkok dwellers have studied or traveled abroad (or have been exposed to Western ways even if they have stayed at home), an American working in Bangkok might find that his Thai coworker collects Beethoven tapes, studies Japanese at night, discusses modern British novels, and knows the lineup of the Chicago Bears.

In Thailand's growing regional centers—such as Phuket (a popular seaside resort with an international clientele) or Chiang Mai (home of two universities and an international airport)— many Thais share the same education and international exposure as do their Bangkok counterparts. The question then becomes: to what extent do the well-traveled Bangkok businesswoman, the Chiang Mai professor with a Cornell Ph.D., and the Phuket hotelier share cultural values with a village farmer pushing a crude plow? But surprising as it may seem at first, they actually share quite a bit, the most important being language (or more precisely, a dialect of the same language). Standard (or "central") Thai is spoken in Bangkok and the rest of the central part of Thailand. In the north, northeast, and south, the first language of the people is their own regional dialect; but many also speak standard Thai as well since it is the medium of instruction in the schools and is used in government offices, by the press, in the movies, and on the radio.

Use of the same language tends to create a similar worldview. Since the same store of linguistic concepts is called on for expressing an idea, and since both have been raised as members of the established social order (albeit in different places in that order), they share an intuitive understanding of how to relate to others in their society.

In short they share an underlying set of Thai attitudes and cultural values. The Bangkokian, however, adds to or modifies this basic set of values as he or she consciously or unconsciously adopts certain Western traits and attitudes and, in a sense, straddles the wide gulf between rural Thailand and the industrialized West. Many Thais have successfully absorbed the best of both worlds and in so doing have contributed to Thailand's push for economic development while helping to maintain the integrity of traditional Thai culture.

In discussing Thai values, it will thus be necessary at times to distinguish certain characteristics which are found generally throughout Thai society from those which are more or less unique to Bangkok and the other cities—or which have undergone modification or virtually disappeared in Bangkok. We will first consider some basic similarities between Thais and Americans. Next we will look at some major differences and then show how these similarities and differences manifest themselves in social relations. Finally, we will relate Thai and American cultural patterns to the business environment to see how attitudes toward work, relations at work, and management procedures reflect the distinctive cultural themes which we have identified.

One final note: it might at times appear that discussion of cultural differences is not worth the effort, for the road to understanding appears fraught with tough-to-articulate nuances and subtle distinctions in degree and timing. But, rather than viewing the quest for understanding in this negative light, it might be better to view it as a mosaic in the making so that as each new piece of information is fitted into the conceptual frame, the patterns of Thai and American culture come into increasingly sharper focus. How detailed and complete a mosaic you eventually fashion will depend, of course, on your own time and interest. It is hoped that this book will at least start you on the way.

2

Basic Similarities

Love of Freedom

One of the most striking similarities between Thais and Americans is their love of freedom, both at the national level—in the sense that they have jealously defended their sovereignty—and at the individual level, where they both place a high premium on personal independence and resist outside control. Both allude to freedom and the bravery necessary to sustain it in their national anthems, both have long histories of freedom from control by outside forces, and both resist attempts by their own social or political institutions to regiment or otherwise restrict them.

In fact, the word *Thai* means free, and the word for *Thailand* (in Thai) means "Land of the Free." This freedom has existed since 1238, when the Thais, who had earlier migrated south from China, overthrew their Khmer masters and established their first kingdom at Sukhothai, located in the north-central region of present-day Thailand. An interesting parallel can be drawn between the American frontiersmen, who pushed westward and escaped—at least temporarily—the yoke of the federal government, and residents of certain Thai principalities, who as recently as the last century were outside the control of the Thai state.

7

Lacking America's economic and military might, Thailand has had to resort to a different weapon in order to preserve her freedom—an astute diplomacy, which has juggled and balanced interests and discerned the ebb and flow of international relations with remarkable sophistication and consummate skill. This diplomatic acumen was initially important during the mid nineteenth century when King Mongkut—harassed by the French on the one side and the British on the other—had to decide "whether to swim up river to make friends with the crocodile or to swim out to sea and hang on to the whale."[1] Eventually treaties were enacted with both the crocodile and the whale as well as with other Western powers, thereby preserving Thailand's traditional sovereignty. This art of diplomacy is reflected in Thai social relations as well and will be discussed in more detail later.

Pragmatism

Pragmatic, realistic, clever, down-to-earth—these are just a few of the terms that could be used to describe both Thais and Americans. Eschewing rigid adherence to any particular ideology, both peoples are extremely adept at cutting through long-winded cant, soberly sizing up the possibilities and problems involved in a particular situation, and then realistically charting an appropriate course of action. Lest this be interpreted as a wholly positive approach to life, let it be said that there is often a fine line between realism and cynicism, cleverness and guile. Thus, Americans have been accused of narrowly pursuing their own self-interest at others' expense, and Thais have been charged with practicing the unreliable policy of bending with the wind.

Be that as it may, there is no doubt that the intense realism and practicality of both peoples have helped them to survive and even prosper in the world. The astute Yankee trader meets his match in the shrewd Siamese diplomat. Thai tales repeatedly have as their moral the warning that one should not be tricked or deceived, and little sympathy is offered those who are. Proverbs caution against a trust too freely given: "An old slave and a loving wife—put not your trust in these." Thais would no doubt wholeheartedly agree with comparable American sayings, such as "A fool and his money are soon parted."

American pragmatism reflects the practical bent of a people more concerned with clearing the forest, building a house, and planting crops than with creating theories as to why they were doing it. This pragmatic instinct meshed well with the demands of a rapidly developing economy in which efficiency and output were in large part determined by the way an entrepreneur could shift and adjust to meet everchanging market conditions. One had to be flexible enough to experiment with different procedures until one that worked was found. No theory or tradition was so sacrosanct that it could not be tinkered with and, when necessary, discarded if it did not produce a practical result. Economic rewards went to the person who could "build a better mousetrap." From pioneer to astronaut, the American has been resourceful, inventive, and above all, pragmatic.

Though Thai pragmatism parallels the practical, realistic American approach, it springs from decidedly different roots. Central to an understanding of Thai pragmatism is a grasp of some of the basic tenets of Buddhism and a knowledge of how the Thais have evolved their own unique type of Buddhism—making even more practical what was already the most practical of religions.

After intense meditation, Buddha enunciated the "Four Noble Truths": All life is sorrow; sorrow is the result of unchecked desire; cessation of desire ends life and sorrow; and such cessation is attained by following the eightfold path of right understanding, right purpose, right speech, right action, right livelihood, right effort, alertness for the truth, and contemplation. This eightfold path is known as "The Middle Way" between extremes of living.

Thus, Buddhism in its very essence is highly practical and realistic, for it is grounded in Buddha's realization of what the human condition actually is, and it prescribes practical steps that can be taken to cope with (and eventually escape from) this condition. Unlike most other religions, it makes no mention of supernatural beings or deities. Instead, it starts with the condition in which human beings find themselves here on earth and then seeks to help them practically and realistically deal with that condition.

But as seemingly practical as this approach was, the Thais changed it, making it less austere and mystical and much more congenial to the Thai temperament. Mystical contemplation and the rigorous discipline needed to transcend this world and eventually attain the somewhat nebulous state (or nonstate) of Nirvana simply did not sit well with the Thai proclivity for present sensuous happiness. So contemplation was deemphasized. Thais generally tend to think in terms of rebirth into better worldly conditions rather than in attaining a hard-to-understand Nirvana. As one Thai professor, Prasert Yamlinfung, has explained it:

> The idea of renunciation of worldliness and the implied negative attitude towards the accumulation of wealth are never taken seriously by most Thai Buddhists as these beliefs run against their values of enjoyment of living in harmony with oneself, others, and nature.

Because they have long emphasized the practical over the theoretical, both Thais and Americans have been accused of being, among other things, superficial and shallow—which is why, so it is argued, they have not produced noted philosophers or great creative thinkers. Persuasive, but not profound; down-to-earth but not earth-shattering—to a certain extent these appear to be valid criticisms, yet pragmatism itself is a philosophy and one that requires considerable worldly wisdom to appreciate and live by. Suffice it to say that this common ground of pragmatism can serve as a solid basis for Thai and American cooperation. Unfettered by rigid ideology or overbearing dogma both peoples can make realistic assessments and flexible adjustments as they search for ways to solve problems of mutual concern.

Dislike of Pomposity

Another characteristic shared by Americans and Thais is their dislike of pomposity and arrogance. Both peoples have finely tuned radar to pick up even a hint of pretension in the air and will be quickly turned off by boastful, self-aggrandizing speech. Americans may try to "take the wind out of the sails" of a particularly offensive egotist, whereas Thais may make the comment (though not to the person directly) concerning a verbose bore, "The water floods the field, but little morning glory grows."

The American distaste for someone who comes on too strong reflects the notion that one should not put on airs or act stuck-up. Such a person may be "taken down a peg or two." All of this indicates a leveling tendency in American society, a constant attempt to make sure that no one pulls rank or lords it over others.

These ideas took shape in the early history of the United States when immigrants—most of whom came from the lower classes of European society—wanted to rid themselves of the mother country's aristocratic stratification. In the United States, one person was to be as good as the next, and thus the preference even today is for an easygoing informality in social relations and a corresponding disdain for one who tries to act like a big shot.

In Thailand the present social structure as well as the historical attitude toward stratification differ greatly from the American pattern. These differences will be discussed in some detail later. The important thing to remember is that despite these differences in social organization, Thais share with Americans a decidedly negative reaction to those they perceive as *thỹy tua* (literally "holding oneself up") in the sense of holding oneself aloof or acting conceited. Like Americans, Thais prefer a relaxed informality in social interaction with friends and enjoy social events that are *pen kan eng* (informal and familiar, where you loosen up and make yourself at home).

Looking at Thais from the outside, this essential similarity in outlook between the two peoples may not initially be perceived, since accompanying (or often preceding) the Thai relaxed informality is an emphasis on polite deference to rank in the form of *wâis* (gestures of respect which consist of placing one's hands together at the breast and bowing) and a general tendency to let those of higher status set the tone for the degree of informality in a gathering.

But the desire for informality and the disdain for pomposity on the part of the Thais is definitely there, as was well captured by Reginald le May in 1930:

> Trust them as a friend, as an equal, and they will open their hearts. Come among them as an official with stern, unbending mien, and they will close their mouths like oysters at the touch.

Freedom-loving, pragmatic, and disdaining pomposity, Thais and Americans share a certain way of looking at the world. Knowing this much about the two peoples, one could predict that in many social and business situations, the Thai and American attitude or response would be remarkably similar. There is, then, a commonality, a basis for mutual understanding that Americans and Thais can build on as they live and work together. Knowing that they share certain fundamental values, Thais and Americans can then begin to discern exactly how and where (and maybe why) they differ in other respects. It is to an analysis of some of these differences that we now turn.

[1] From King Mongkut's letter to the Thai Embassy in France which has been translated into English in *Mongkut: King of Siam* by Abbot Low Moffat. Ithaca, NY: Cornell University Press, 1962.

3

ഌ

Key Differences

The Relationship of Land and People

The early immigrants to the North American continent from Europe found a vast, harsh wilderness which they had to contend with and master if they were to survive. Winters, especially, were stern and unforgiving, and the pioneers had to struggle constantly to withstand the cruelties to which nature subjected them. The early Thais likewise immigrated to their present homeland; they came from southern China. But the environment awaiting them was not a harsh one. The weather was warm the year round, and the land and water teemed with a wide variety of plant and animal life. The central plain, which was to become the country's heartland, was a particularly fertile flatland, perfect for rice cultivation.

The spirit of this early era is neatly capsulized in a stone inscription authored in 1283 by a famous Thai monarch, King Ram Kamhaeng: "This land of Thai is good. In the waters are fish; in the fields is rice.... Coconut groves abound in this land.... Jackfruit abounds in this land. Mango trees abound in this land.... Whoever wants to play, plays. Whoever wants to laugh, laughs. Whoever wants to sing, sings." Accommodation to such an environment was clearly not difficult. People had only to harmonize with what was around them, conform to the rhythm of the seasons, and enjoy the bounty which nature provided.

Nature was not viewed in such a benevolent light by the early Americans. A foe rather than a friend, the physical environment seemed a huge obstacle course which people had to somehow outwit. Harmony was out of the question. Control was the answer. The power of the rivers had to be harnessed; the wilderness had to be tamed. The attitude that a person is separate from and master of the environment persists, for Americans even today speak of conquering space. Americans, then, view nature as merely a background for mankind. Asians, conversely, have tended to view humans as more a part of, or even as a background to, nature.

Along with the American view of people's dominance over the environment goes a strong emphasis on measurability. The world is seen as having dimensions that can be quantified—by an arbitrarily assigned numerical value, sometimes simply as "first or last," "least or most." Ability, performance and even intelligence are measured by statistics. In everything from weather forecasts to sports broadcasts, Americans are bombarded with figures. Since it is something they take for granted, they are generally not aware that most other cultures find this emphasis on statistics puzzling if not amusing.

Treatment of the Thai and American views of nature would be incomplete without some allusion to the religious beliefs which not only helped to shape people's attitudes toward their environment but were also reinforced by people's experiences with that environment. Simply stated, the heavy Calvinistic strain running through early American religious thought quickened the pace with which a person struggled with the surroundings. The morally good person was the hardworking, timesaving, frugal individual. For keeping one's nose to the earthly grindstone, one would be rewarded with heavenly salvation. A person had but one chance and had to make the best of it or face the unpleasant prospect of the eternal damnation awaiting those who loafed, squandered, or otherwise shirked the call to constant toil.

The Buddhist influence on Thai thinking could hardly have been more different. Life was not viewed as a one-shot, all-or-nothing proposition. Instead the great Wheel of Existence ensured that each individual would have many lives, returning again and again to earth to be rewarded (by birth in a higher position than in the previous life) or punished (by birth in a lower position), depending upon the accumulated good and evil of past lives. Given such a long-range view of existence, the Thai obviously did not feel the compulsion experienced by the American to make every moment count. Relatively content with a comfortable life, the Thai saw no need to struggle with the environment, and the Thai's religious beliefs provided no rationale for such a struggle.

Given their orientation to nature, Americans have viewed germs, droughts, mosquitoes, and even earthquakes as essentially subject to their control, as problems calling for discussion, mobilization of resources, and appropriate action. Thais, on the other hand, have tended to treat such natural disasters as flood and crop failures simply as matters beyond their control—as normal, if regrettable, aspects of recurrent natural cycles.

The American pattern has fostered economic development; the traditional Thai outlook has not. In aggressively attacking nature, Americans have been able to industrialize rapidly and to enjoy a high standard of material comfort. In living peacefully with nature, Thais (at least in the rural areas) have experienced no massive drive to development; they nevertheless have enjoyed a high standard of contentment. Americans have only recently begun to question this all-out drive for economic development as they have found it polluting their environment. The ecology movement indicates that Americans are now searching for ways to live more in harmony with nature. At the same time, Thais are making considerable strides in economic and rural development. As Americans strive to restore a natural balance and Thais push for economic development, it is clear that there is a high potential for mutually beneficial relationships.

Authority and Power

To Americans, authority is something to be challenged, and power something to be suspicious of, fragmented, and weakened. This Anglo-American approach to power, embodied in the assertion that power corrupts and absolute power corrupts absolutely, permeates the American political and social fabric to such an extent that Americans would scarcely think that power could be viewed in any other light.

Jefferson's famous declaration, "That government governs best which governs least" and the emphasis on separation and division of powers at all levels of government reflect this deep-seated American distrust of power generally, particularly its concentration or centralization.

The traditional Thai view of power and authority is a mirror-image reversal. Authority and power have been considered natural to the human condition. Authority and power derive from the moral and ethical excellence of those who hold it. The presence of power indicates that its holder has accumulated merit in a previous life and now enjoys the fruits of past superior behavior. At the pinnacle of power stands the monarchy, which is highly revered in Thailand. Despite the deference which Thais have historically shown to the king, there has never existed the Western notion that he is "lording it over" the people in an oppressive sense. In fact, in Southeast Asia generally, just the opposite view is held. The wealth and power of the ruler and the splendor of the court and temples have been considered a symbol of cultural well-being and a projection of the peasantry's own greatness.

The traditional organization of Thai society was built on lines of command. The king was the ultimate source of authority with an intricate hierarchy of nobles under him. In all relationships there were distinct superior and subordinate roles. The king ruled over, in a sense owned, not only all the land within the kingdom but all the people as well, for he was both *phrá câw paèndin* (Lord of the Land) and also *câw chiwít* (Lord of Life).

It is extremely difficult for Americans to understand the deep loyalty, respect, and love that Thais have for their king because there is no personage that occupies a similar position in their own frame of reference. Comparing the king to the president of the United States is inadequate, for the latter is seen as a "first among equals," a capable citizen who just happens temporarily to hold high office. Thus, Americans feel free to criticize, caricature, and even vilify their president if they believe his actions so warrant.

Such denigration of the king would be unthinkable to a Thai, and no greater cultural sin could be committed by an American in Thailand than to insult or even speak of the king in any but the most respectful terms. To do so would seriously antagonize any Thais who heard it (or of it) and possibly make the rest of the American's stay in Thailand a very unhappy one, if not a shortened one.

Thais themselves do not criticize the king, particularly in public settings. Such an offense is punishable by law. Recently, a Thai politician was speaking before a village group far from Bangkok. He made some negative remarks about the royal family which, in the U.S., would have been considered tame. But in Thailand word of his disrespect got back to Bangkok and the politician was charged with *lèse majesté* and sent to jail.

Some foreigners make the mistake of thinking that their own casual, disrespectful comments about the monarchy go unnoticed. They don't. One foreign family hosted a dinner party in their own home and hired extra waiters from a local hotel. During the dinner the conversation turned to the monarchy and some lighthearted, if slightly disrespectful, comments were made. The next day Thai investigators, no doubt tipped off by the hotel staff, appeared at their door to caution the foreigners against such unacceptable behavior. While it is unusual for foreigners to be approached thus in their homes since the Thais generally live and let live, the fact remains that in Thailand royalty must not be referred to disrespectfully.

All of this does not imply that His Majesty King Bhumibol Adulyadej is not deserving of such respect. By all accounts the king is a serious monarch, sincerely dedicated to the welfare of his country. He makes frequent trips to rural areas of Thailand to stay in touch with his people and to observe development projects. December 5, 1987, was the king's sixtieth birthday. All of Bangkok became a fairyland of lights to celebrate the event, and virtually every major company, Thai and foreign, did something special to mark it, such as making a large donation to a charitable cause, dedicating a cultural building, or publishing a book highlighting Thailand's art and culture.

The relationship of King Bhumibol and his subjects represents the ideal Thai senior/junior, higher/lower relationship. The king is a person who is genuinely worthy of respect and has a fatherly concern for his subjects. In turn his subjects show their respect for him. Their reverence is based on traditional etiquette and respect, not fear.

It is clear then that American and Thai attitudes toward authority and power differ fundamentally. Though it may be difficult for either people to fully appreciate the historical forces which have led to this difference in outlook, it is important that they are at least aware of the wide gulf which separates them over this issue. Thais must try to grasp the reasons behind Americans' distrust of power, and Americans must try to understand why Thais do not share that distrust. The American pattern of decentralized power and the Thai system of deference to authority will obviously affect both people's thinking in many areas of their lives, including their approach to business. More about that later.

Social Structure

Americans are taught as school children that "all men are created equal." What's more, this somewhat debatable proposition has been enshrined in the Declaration of Independence as well as in the American psyche as a "self-evident truth." Leaving behind European aristocracies, the early Americans tried to insure that all persons—regardless of birth—would be given equal treatment before the law and an equal chance to participate in the developing economy.

This notion of equality has always been an ideal rather than an accurate description of social reality (the founding fathers themselves apparently intended equality only for white, property-owning males). There can be little doubt that, consistent with that ideal, political and social equality have been gradually extended over the two hundred years of the Republic's existence. More precisely, the emphasis has always been equality of *opportunity* rather than equality of rewards. If this were not the case, the value of egalitarianism would clash directly with the value of liberty, the notion that from an equal starting point one should be able to go as far as one's interests and abilities allow.

Egalitarianism is instilled at an early age in Americans, who as children typically have a significant say in decisions which affect them—what to eat for breakfast, what TV show to watch, etc. As they cajole, persuade, reason, or negotiate, parents tend to treat their children as if they were merely smaller and less sophisticated versions of adults. The parents, implicitly or explicitly, often reject the idea that their authority is supreme simply because they are adults. By the standards of most cultures of the world, such treatment seems rather bizarre, but it makes perfect sense to the egalitarian-minded American.

American egalitarianism can come as a rude jolt to Thai (and other) visitors to the United States, often manifesting itself in interaction with Americans in such service occupations as store clerks, waitresses, and taxi drivers. Accustomed to a certain amount of consideration and respect back home because of position, a Thai may be taken aback when the American service person fails to behave in a solicitous, deferential manner. To further complicate things, the service person will expect to be treated as an equal, feel free to offer opinions on everything from sports to politics, and address the visitor (with characteristic American informality) as "buddy," "mister," "lady," or simply "you."

It takes considerable patience and understanding to recognize that, in American terms, the service person is acting in a perfectly normal way, treating the visitor no differently than he or she would a fellow American. Believing in the essential equality of human beings, people in service positions are disinclined to show overt respect for others based on their status alone.

If egalitarianism is the central theme in the American social structure, it is hierarchic relations which are at the heart of Thai society. In virtually every social situation there is a distinction between superior and inferior positions. It is important to note that traditionally those of low status have never viewed such a social system as particularly unreasonable or severe. Rather, they have tended to feel that those who have status and authority derive them to a certain extent from their moral and ethical excellence, having, in the Buddhist context, accumulated merit from a previous life.

A systematically imposed hierarchical structure was achieved in the kingdom in the fifteenth century, when royal princes were given titles which showed how many generations they were removed from the kingly forebears, and commoner officials were given ranks which indicated their status or degree of dignity. One had to show the necessary respect to those who were higher in the social order and could extract a corresponding measure of deference from those below.

Anthropologist Michael Moerman has summarized the basic Thai hierarchical pattern in this way:

> Younger-elder, child-parent, layman-priest, peasant-official—bonds between inferior and superior compose the family, the village, and the nation. In return for the service and respect of his subordinate, the superior gives protection and leadership. In none of these relationships is there any provision for the inferior to challenge the wisdom of his superior, to express ideas of which his superior might disapprove, to provide direction to his superior's actions.

An important aspect of the relationship between subordinate and superior is the notion (which dates from the fifteenth century) that a person should have an influential individual on whom he can *phyyng* (depend) for assistance in coping with life's vagaries. The depth of this client-patron relationship varies with the degree of mutual affection and trust. Benefits flow both ways since the patron can also call on the client to provide certain services, and, in Buddhist terms, the help rendered to the client affords the patron the opportunity to achieve merit (and thus increase one's chance of a higher position in the next life).

In 1988 reactions to the death of Chin Sophonpanich provided clear evidence that such patron-client relationships are still alive and well in Thailand. Khun ("Mr.") Chin was a Chinese immigrant to Thailand who founded the Bangkok Bank, the largest bank in Southeast Asia, and became one of the world's wealthiest men. Despite his enormous wealth and power, he continued to play his part in the time-honored patron/client relationship. The *Bangkok Post* quoted one of his longtime employees saying: "Khun Chin was a special kind of boss. He never punished his subordinates for errors they made. Instead, he gave encouragement, instructing us to learn from our mistakes. His subordinates repaid this kindness by selflessly dedicating themselves to their work."

Said another subordinate: "I remember how Khun Chin would always join his subordinates at mealtimes. Despite his rank, seniority, and wealth, he was always informal and at ease with us, joining us for meals to ask how things were going with us and our families. He believed in giving. He believed that once he helped us with our families' well-being, we would give our best in performing our duty."

The incredible complexity of the Thai hierarchy is reflected in the elaborate system of pronouns which exists in the Thai language to enable a person in any situation to show just the right amount of respect, deference, and intimacy. It took one linguist sixty-four pages to describe in detail exactly how all the forms are used. Compare this with the few sentences that would be needed to explain the use of *I, you, he, she, we,* and *they* in English.

Look, for example, at some pronouns for *I* and *you* which are commonly used in everyday life in Thailand. A secretary who is thirty years old is referred to as *pî* (older one), while she refers to her twenty-eight-year-old fellow secretary as *nong* (younger one). A man uses the pronoun *phŏm* for "I." When addressing a waitress one might use the pronoun *ňu* (mouse). Other ways of saying "you" indicate a respect for position. A doctor is called *khun mǎw*; a professor is called *acharn*.

Americans in Thailand have mixed reactions to the Thai hierarchical system. Most of the time a senior executive of an American company will enjoy the respect and deference that is shown to him because of his position. But at times he may also feel slightly uncomfortable at the polite formality with which his Thai subordinates treat him.

A young American academic teaching at a Thai university might have a different set of reactions. She might enjoy the respect her students show her but feel frustrated at their unwillingness (based on years of conditioning) to challenge her ideas and participate in intellectual debate out of deference to her respected position as a professor. Yet, in dealing with her fellow professors she might bridle at the strong sense of hierarchy in which she, as a young person with only a master's degree, is always treated as a junior by her Thai Ph.D. colleagues, despite her obvious intellectual ability and knowledge.

Though the different stations in the hierarchy are relatively fixed, this does not mean that an individual is forever chained to an assigned slot. Rather, there has been a relatively high degree of social mobility; indeed, several kings have emerged from humble backgrounds to assume the throne. This fluidity of social position prevents hardening of the hierarchic arteries and gives to Thai society a certain sense of flexibility within an enduring cultural framework. Despite the obvious emphasis given to status and position in individual face-to-face relationships, there is an underlying idea—not unlike the American concept of equality of opportunity—which allows individuals to climb the social ladder and attain some of the highest social positions of the land.

The American pattern of egalitarianism is seen as being rather stultifying; since there exists only *I* and *you* for ordinary conversation, there is no way for one to express one's own unique relationship to another individual. President, priest, professor or plumber— all must be addressed with the monotonous "you" by the egalitarian-minded American. When during World War II the Thai premier advocated reducing pronouns to one set for expressing the "I-you" relationship, the move was seen by some as an assault on freedom and democracy!

Concept of Time

Americans say, "My watch is *running* fast (or slow)." Thais say literally, "My watch is *walking* fast (or slow)." This one simple sentence says quite a bit about the relative pace of the two societies. Time to Americans is a fast-moving river they must run to keep up with; time and tide, as the saying goes, wait for no man. Time to Thais is a slow-moving pool, which they can gradually walk around. Americans consider time as a straight line, a road stretching into the future along which one progresses. Thais, and Asians generally, tend to view time as a circle with recurring phases: one season follows the next, one life leads into another, one king's reign is followed by another.

With their lineal view of time, Americans divide up the future into discrete segments; they then plan, schedule, and compartmentalize these segments. This planned, compartmentalized approach to time is reflected in the importance of advance notice or "lead time" in the United States. One normally does not just drop in on someone—either at home or at the office—as might be done in Thailand. This lineal, scheduled approach causes Americans to value promptness highly and treat time as a material object which they can "spend," "save," or "waste." This emphasis on the productive use of one's time has been stressed by Americans to a point unequalled elsewhere in the world, except perhaps in Switzerland and northern Germany.

Another aspect of the American concept of time, as noted especially by Edward T. Hall in *The Silent Language,* is the *monochronic* nature of American behavior. This simply means that Americans like to do one thing at a time and feel uncomfortable if they are interrupted while in the midst of one activity. Americans will thus try to schedule appointments so that they will see only one person at a time.

To Americans time is money, but in Thailand—particularly in the rural areas—time is not generally equated with earning a living. Most farmers do not think of themselves as having lost money if they're forced to waste time. In fact, they do not appear to have a strong notion of "wasting" time at all. Living close to nature's cycles and wishing to avoid the anxieties of preparing for the future or lamenting the past causes the Thai villager to live mostly in the present, to enjoy above all the passing moment.

Americans, on the other hand, tend to emphasize the future, believing that through present discipline and labor, a rosier tomorrow will dawn. In fact, some Americans seem to live in a state of perpetual deferred gratification and would be lost without their calendars, appointment books, and schedules.

Even so, their view of the future is still somewhat limited; essentially it is the *foreseeable* future that concerns them, as opposed to the Asian concept of the future which may involve centuries. Thus, the "long-term" to the American is five or ten years, and this is reflected in American planning practices.

Related to the different concepts of time in the two cultures is the sense of urgency that prevails in American society—typified by the omnipresence of wailing sirens. Thais newly arrived in the U.S. find it hard to believe that so many matters have to be tended to at such breakneck speed and accompanied by such ear-shattering noise. It clashes strongly with the Thai saying, "Hurry, but hurry slowly," though among urban, Westernized Thais these attitudes are changing.

The Rhythm and Pattern of Life

We have seen a certain horizontal orientation in American society—a constant attempt to distribute and disperse power and authority to as broad an extent as possible and an accompanying tendency to level differences in status by insisting on an informal egalitarianism in social relations. Thailand, in contrast, has more of a vertical orientation, characterized by a concentration of power at the top of the social structure and a hierarchical social order featuring a series of superior/subordinate relationships.

It is time now to relate these differing orientations to specific aspects of daily life in the two societies, for one of the hardest things for an American in Thailand or a Thai in America to understand is the rhythm or pattern which prevails in the other society. Things seem to happen irregularly or haphazardly; many things in fact just don't seem to make sense in terms of the familiar values of the home culture.

As they encountered this very different rhythm in Thai life, some American anthropologists were led to describe Thai society as "loosely structured" in the sense that there did not seem to be many binding rules which would lead to predictable behavior. Generalizations concerning the underlying structure of society seemed impossible since in so many instances individual Thais just seemed to go their own way or, in current terminology, "do their own thing." Other anthropologists, while agreeing that the Thais did manifest considerable individualistic behavior, were troubled by the "loosely structured" label, particularly in light of the highly complex structure of the Thai hierarchical social order.

Our task, then, is to take these two opposing strands which run through Thai society—great freedom and diversity of individual behavior on the one hand and scrupulous attention to the demands of the social hierarchy on the other—and try to weave them together so that a clearer rhythm or pattern will emerge. The next step will be to contrast this pattern with the one which character-izes American society.

Start by taking a rubber band. Stretch it as tightly as you can; then release it so it slackens. Now stretch it tight again; now release. This will give you some sense of the rhythm of Thai life. For there is a constant interplay of these two extremes—a tautness or rigidity when an important vertical relationship is involved and a corresponding slackening or looseness once the demands of this relationship have been fulfilled.

Three students may be out on a leisurely stroll and then chance to meet their teacher or another respected elder. They will immediately act in an appropriately deferential manner by giving the proper hand salute (*wâi*), using the correct pronouns to refer to themselves and the teacher, and transforming their previous boisterous conduct into a soft, gentle picture of decorum. All of this will be done automatically, for the proper behavior in such a situation is so structured that it requires no conscious effort to bring it about. Once the teacher has passed, they will saunter on their easygoing way.

Or an office worker may be chatting idly with some colleagues when suddenly she receives an order from her supervisor. She will "snap to," race to carry out the order, and then pick up where she left off with her coworkers. Again, the conduct in the situation is prescribed; there is no room for deviation. In like manner, a villager may drop everything he is doing to fulfill an important reciprocal obligation to a friend or patron, then just as quickly return to his relaxed routine.

Whenever there is an important vertical interaction at stake, usually one involving a show of respect, obedience, or reciprocity, both parties—superior and subordinate—have a finely honed intuitive sense of exactly how to act in the particular situation. They have, in effect, internalized the complex web of the Thai social hierarchy and know precisely how much deference the superior is entitled to and exactly how this respect is to be manifested by the subordinate. But once they have performed the rigidly prescribed conduct called for in their encounter, they are free to go their own ways until another superior/subordinate situation arises.

If the rhythm of Thai life can (at least superficially) be captured by analogy to a rubber band, the corresponding image in American life would be a piece of string held fairly taut at all times. Never would there be the rigidity comparable to that of the Thai hierarchical interaction. Yet, never would there be the same degree of looseness or personal freedom which the Thai pattern fosters either.

In the U.S. there are internal as well as external constraints operating to insure that the pace of life does not slacken. Internal constraints (that is, those operating within the individual) would include an ingrained work ethic, a sense of guilt, and a belief that time should be used productively. External constraints (that is, those operating in society which impinge on the individual) consist mainly of laws, rules, and rigid procedures of one kind or another which tend to rein in free-spirited impulses. Everywhere they turn, Americans are met head-on by these confining, controlling regulations: don't walk, don't litter, keep off the grass, show two ID cards, observe the speed limit, have this document notarized, etc.

This relatively legalistic approach is so much a part of the daily life of Americans that they can scarcely think the world could be ordered otherwise. But it is clearly not the pattern which prevails in many other countries, among them Thailand. This is not to say that the Thais have no rules; it's just that they often have a more relaxed manner of dealing with them, as illustrated in these words by one Thai social scientist, Adul Wichiencharoen, who called his people "bad law-abiders":

> They never take rules, regulations or law seriously either as law enforcer or law abider... [Violations] are committed despite the fact that the actors know very well that they are violating rules and regulations. Violation of law and order is so frequent that sometimes Thai people take it as part of life.

But in the case of Thai attitudes toward laws, the principle of the elastic band can again be applied. On the one hand, Thais are very loose about laws and regulations. They may display a *mai pen rai* attitude in some cases. *Mai pen rai* is a commonly used phrase in Thailand which means "never mind" in the sense of "Don't worry about it. It's OK." This phrase smooths over uncomfortable situations big and small. But at other times, Thais can be very concerned about laws and regulations. An American in business in Thailand would do well to ask the advice of a trusted and perceptive Thai colleague to decipher when flexibility or when rigidity is called for.

One American businessman comments: "Where Thai society has done best is where they have been flexible and rules have been treated as fluid at the upper levels of decision making. Sometimes upper-echelon Thais in the bureaucracy do not clearly state the rules they are following so that they are free to respond flexibly and to make their best judgments as situations arise. In many situations this is highly admirable and things work out for the best."

But in other circumstances, he notes, Thai bureaucrats, particularly low-ranking ones, can be extremely inflexible. There may be specific regulations governing, for example, the filing of a business report with the government. While many people might ignore the filing requirement, figuring there is no efficient system to catch violators, it is possible that one could be caught and prosecuted to the letter of the law. "Before there is a well-documented trail of evidence against the violator a small amount of money could take care of the whole thing; but once there is a well-documented case, the violator may be subject to full punishment," he says.

Viewing the two societies in terms of the rubber band versus the string helps explain many of the confusions and negative comments which arise when a Thai first comes to America or an American first enters Thailand. Thais often complain that Americans do not understand and cannot appreciate anything lofty like their monarchy. In their terms American society seems generally lacking in authority, respect, and deference. But this is because they are looking in vain for instances of the tightly stretched rubber band, the accustomed superior/subordinate relationships, and are not realizing that the American pattern simply does not allow for them.

On the other hand, Thais will often note that American life seems more demanding, enervating, and relentless, which is not only disappointing but also paradoxical since the ingredient which would (in their terms) stimulate this behavior—strong vertical respect relationships—is missing. Where, they wonder, does this inexorable drive come from in a society which seems so superficially informal? Again, they fail to appreciate that it is a string, not a rubber band, which is representing American behavior; that is, they do not fully understand the internal and external constraints mentioned earlier which generally do not allow the behavioral freedom to which Thais are accustomed.

Americans are similarly bewildered when they first go to Thailand. Since most of the time they are observing periods when the rubber band is slackened, they see the Thais as relaxed, pleasant people who don't seem to have the same level of self-discipline and drive that Americans do. Then suddenly they are caught off guard when a hierarchical demand is placed on a Thai and he responds with a seriousness and apparent obsequiousness which seem rigid and formal in the extreme. Now, the American wonders, what could have caused that rapid transformation? For not only does the deferential conduct clash with the American's basically egalitarian bent, but it also seems to clash violently with the stereotype he had just been developing of the easygoing Thai.

In American terms, the level of sheer enjoyment experienced by the Thais seems almost obscene, for it violates the American's notion of disciplined responsibility. At the same time, the Thais' conduct in superior/subordinate situations seems wrong by standards of American egalitarianism. Both appear extreme to the American because they involve such a radical swing between an attitude that is relaxed to the point of carelessness and behavior that reflects a rigid and energetic adherence to a social norm. This kind of fluctuation—which may be compared to a runner who alternates sprinting and running—is confusing, if not incomprehensible, to Americans who function at a steadier, sometimes relentless pace more like the long-distance runner.

One American university lecturer in Thailand found himself annoyed by the lack of advance planning in his department. Students did not look ahead when preparing important papers, and faculty members left the details of an important conference to the last minute. "Even the VIP guests were invited just a few days before," he complained. But when the big moment arrives, Thais can put out enormous effort. One American executive was amazed by the energy his Thai staff poured into the promotion of a new product—flooding dealerships all over the country with publicity materials virtually overnight. On another occasion, the staff were presented with a mandate to update a complex computer system. "Once they understood the need for the change, they turned on to the project with dramatic, quick work which came in under budget. They were hardworking, capable, and committed," said the boss.

Americans working in Thailand cannot suddenly transform themselves into sprinters, but they should consider adopting a pace that will be more congruent with the one around them. A relentless, driving manner will simply lead to frustration since it will alienate Thai coworkers and will not succeed in accomplishing the desired mission. Similarly, Thais working with Americans or studying in the United States will have to realize that they are perhaps among long-distance runners and, to some extent, will have to adjust their pace accordingly.

While, as we can see, the rhythm and tempo of the two societies are extremely different, it is likely that in the Thai business environment they will grow closer in coming years. One senior Thai executive notes that in the last ten years, more and more Thai students have studied business in the U.S., where the emphasis is on planning, control, decision making, accountability, and, especially, the constant productive use of time. These students bring Western management techniques into practice in the Thai business environment. Also, as Thai firms grow, there is a greater recognition of Western techniques and a greater motivation to operate along lines that will make them competitive internationally.

4

Social Relations

Individualism and Awareness of Others

We mentioned earlier that both Thais and Americans love and have long experienced freedom, both at the national and at the individual level; both look for ways to increase personal independence, resist regimentation, and generally try to avoid outside control over their lives. Accordingly, both peoples have been described as individualistic, a word originally coined by the French aristocrat, Alexis de Tocqueville, in the 1830s to describe the "peculiar" nature of American behavior.

Interestingly enough, the word for *individualism* has only recently been coined in Thai; but its absence has not prevented a long line of anthropologists from referring to the Thais as individualistic. Indeed, the term does not seem inappropriate, for in many ways the individualistic tendencies manifested by the Thais parallel those displayed by Americans. In one important respect, however, the individualism of the two peoples seems to be of a different emotional hue. We will deal with this difference after we have first looked at some of the similarities.

Americans have long spoken admiringly of "rugged individualists," and their folklore is filled with tales of those who have struggled against the physical environment, their humble birth, or other substantial obstacles to mold themselves into successful politicians, entrepreneurs, athletes, or whatever. The epitome would probably be Abraham Lincoln, the backwoods boy who studied by candlelight in a small cabin, became president of his country, and has been enshrined in a memorial on the Potomac as well as in the minds and hearts of his countrymen.

That this theme endures is illustrated by the popularity of the film *Rocky*, the man whose "whole life was a hundred-to-one shot." American songs like "King of the Road" and "Don't Fence Me In" reflect the American's need for room, for open spaces—both physical and psychic. John F. Kennedy was able to play on this deeply ingrained American attitude when he spoke of his administration as the "New Frontier."

Thais can readily identify with this self-reliant search for independence. Like Americans, Thais generally believe that people should look first to themselves, to their own intellectual and material resources, to solve a problem. To do otherwise would be weak and foolish. A strong religious base underlies both people's attitudes. In the no-nonsense Calvinism that has long colored American thinking, each individual has had to work out his own salvation: "The Lord helps those who help themselves." The Buddhist precept is similar: "By oneself one is purified." Thais thus say in everyday speech, "Do good, receive good; do evil, receive evil." It's up to you.

Neither Americans nor Thais have the strong sense of lineage or the feeling of ancestry that is characteristic of such peoples as the Chinese, Japanese, and Vietnamese. In both societies the primary orientation is toward members of one's immediate family, although the Thai sense of "immediate" would probably be somewhat broader than the American, reaching out to include more members of the so-called extended family (uncles, aunts, cousins, etc.). But in neither case would there be as binding a system of obligation to extended family or community as might exist in more communal or group-centered societies. Nor would there be a strongly felt need for a formal link between generations in the Chinese sense. Indeed, family names did not exist in Thailand until 1916, when they were established by royal decree; and Americans, as pointed out earlier, purposely tried to avoid the stratification by class and family that they felt was the base of European society.

Nevertheless, despite a certain individualistic quality to Thai behavior, individualism has generally been played down by Thai culture in favor of group harmony, including especially close family ties and smooth interpersonal relations.

Many Thai young adults, whether still students or already married, live with their parents in an extended family compound and accept parental influence on their decisions. Some Thais who have been educated in the U.S. and acquired a taste of independence find it difficult at first when they come back to Thailand and are expected to live with their family and follow the advice of their elders. While Thais have the freedom to follow a wide variety of lifestyles—from banker to artist to politician—once the Thai is in a certain milieu, he or she generally tries to fit into that environment and get along harmoniously with the group.

Socialization in group harmony begins at an early age in Thailand, just as pressure to think independently begins early in the U.S. In both cases the societies are trying to encourage their young to act maturely according to the values of the society. Thai children are not, on the whole, taught to think independently or develop individualistic characteristics which will distinguish one individual from another. They are not taught to bring up contrasting views or challenge another's thoughts, particularly if that person is a teacher or someone in a senior position. American children, by contrast, are taught to think independently and to distinguish themselves from the crowd. These differences in cultural conditioning show up regularly in Thai-U.S. interaction.

American lecturers in Thai universities repeatedly comment on the reluctance of Thai students to speak up in class. "They tend to respect whatever the teacher says," one commented. "My big challenge is to try to stimulate a response or a debate. I try to raise contradictory points, or even make outrageous statements, just to get a response."

Another American professor lamented the tendency of Thai students to look over one another's shoulders during tests and to plagiarize papers. "I gave a closed book exam to see what people had learned," he recalled. "Everyone looked over the shoulder of the other guy. I was outraged. But I backed down and began to realize that this is the system. The group does as well as the best person in the group. It's laudable in a way. The Thais try to help their buddies."

An American businessman in Thailand pointed out the reluctance of Thais to stand out in a crowd in order to distinguish themselves at work, especially if they are junior staffers. "In an American company, when we are looking for potential leaders we look for ambition, assertiveness, a willingness to stick one's neck out on behalf of the organization. These very same qualities that Americans value highly are looked at with suspicion in Thailand, particularly in a young person. The result is that in Thailand we have a cadre of very good middle managers, but a real leader is a very rare individual."

This variance in how Thais and Americans manifest their individualism in everyday social interaction comes about in significant degree because of the differences we have already noted in social structure, the egalitarianism of Americans on the one hand and the hierarchy of Thai society on the other (along with a difference in the way emotions are expressed in the two cultures, which is discussed in detail below).

According to the American concept of equality of opportunity, each person supposedly starts out life with an equal chance for success. How far that person goes will ultimately be up to him or her; family background or inherited wealth by themselves are supposed to be of little assistance in establishing a reputation. Americans, then, are in a sense born without a position in society. They must acquire a position (or status) by dint of their own efforts; Americans thus speak of carving out one's niche in society by personal effort.

In so doing, the person is gradually establishing an identity. This process of self-definition is often not easy, and thus Americans write and counsel each other continuously about the "search for identity," "the identity crisis," etc. If one can successfully establish an identity and carve out a niche which is accorded respect by society, that person is said to be "self-fulfilled." If one fails to do so, he or she is said to be "alienated." The goal of self-fulfillment and the corresponding problem of alienation are discussed endlessly in American life and letters.

Just as the assertive character of American individualism springs naturally from the egalitarian social order, so also does what might be called "nonassertive" individualism grow out of the Thai hierarchical social pattern. Implicit in such a system is the notion of inequality; thus, a person always knows, so to speak, where he or she stands.

A Thai knows who is in a superior position and the amount of deference that must be shown; likewise, the Thai is aware of subordinates in the social order and the respect that can be expected from them. The system not only allows for social mobility (a person could be born a peasant and end up prime minister), but at the same time provides a well-defined role at every station in the hierarchy.

For example, as Thais move up the social ladder, they always move into slots where the roles of superiors and subordinates are well established and well defined. Like Americans, they strive to better their social position. But unlike Americans, Thais will not be so concerned with identity, self-definition, or self-fulfillment, for at each rung of the hierarchy there is an established "definition" already there, simply to be filled. One need only move into the slot to experience the shift in superior-subordinate relationships and the corresponding shift in appropriate hand salutes and pronominal references. Identity is, in effect, pinned on with the new badge of rank.

Actually the use of the term *identity* in the Thai context is somewhat misleading, for it is a Western psychological term that was coined in Thai (*èkalǎksanà*) only a decade ago by a Thai anthropologist; but the word is virtually unknown outside social science circles. This is not to say that Thais do not form identities, for it is undoubtedly a universal human process. But their hierarchical social order has allowed them to do so without the gnawing introspection which the American egalitarian order has fostered.

Just as self-expressive, assertive individualism is implanted in American children at an early age in order to prepare them to cope with the demands of their egalitarian social system, so Thai children are taught to be obedient, polite, and subdued, so that they mesh smoothly into their own hierarchical social fabric.

This difference between American assertive and Thai nonassertive behavior can be seen in clothing styles, body movements, and emotional expressiveness. These will be treated in more depth in subsequent sections. In general, the American's more ostentatious apparel; informal, assertive, body movements; and forceful, direct, emotional expression stand out in sharp contrast to the more subdued Thai dress, physical mannerisms, and modes of expression.

Americans in Thailand would thus do well to tone down their general behavior to some extent in order to conform to the softer, subtler texture of Thai life. Otherwise, sooner or later they will find almost inevitably that they have done or said something needlessly offensive—by Thai standards. Conversely, when dealing with Americans or living in the U.S., Thais would be well advised to tone up their behavior to some degree, to learn to speak and act somewhat more assertively. Encountering someone acting in a subdued, deferential manner can be quite unsettling for Americans, who may also associate quietness with ignorance, since in America well-informed people are expected to develop independent opinions and express them directly and forcefully.

Status

Given the Thai hierarchical system with the monarch as the zenith of power and prestige, it should not be surprising that status has traditionally been correlated directly with how far one stood in the social order from the king. Nobles rendered service to the king in return for his protection and rewards. The nobles in turn had similar symbiotic relationships with their clients, and so on down the line. As we have seen, Buddhism too played an important role in this system. Ultimately, however, in evaluating an individual's status, the key factor was his control of manpower, the number of clients he possessed.

Though the formal administrative structures have obviously changed drastically since those feudal times, many of the old values persist. Thus, royal titles still hold prestige value (although not as much as in former times), and most people continue to view government service as the leading road to status and power. As a government official, one is serving the country and the king; in fact, the Thai word for *civil servant* or *government official* (*khâarâchakan*) literally means "servant of the king." One of the rewards, of course, of being a high-ranking government official is that one has many subordinates or underlings—*luuk náwng* in Thai.

This underlying dichotomy between two unequal positions— whether it be noble/peasant, patron/client, or simply superior/ subordinate—is capsulized in the Thai expression that there must be "a little finger and a thumb" in all social relations. Thus, very few Thais have social equals, whether it be because of age difference, family role, or occupational status. Even twins born a few minutes apart have different statuses because of their minuscule difference in age. In fact there are no words in Thai corresponding to the English *brother* and *sister*. Instead, it must be *older* or *younger brother*, *older* or *younger sister*.

When one Thai meets another for the first time, each must quickly and astutely ascertain the other's proper status in order to use the appropriately deferential language and personal pronouns and to treat each other according to the status accorded his or her position.

An American woman working in Bangkok was planning a business trip to Udorn in the north of Thailand and made extensive plans by telephone with a Thai professional of similar rank whom she had never met before. Arriving at the Udorn airport, she was met by the Thai. One of his first questions was, "What year did you graduate from high school?"

"His question seemed so out of place at the time," she recalled, "but later I realized that he was just trying to place me in the hierarchy as quickly as possible."

Occasionally, selecting the proper pronoun can pose a problem, for in some instances it may be impossible to pick a form which shows neither too much nor too little deference. Take, for example, the case of a young woman who wishes to address a man who is approximately her age and whom she has just met. The first person pronoun, *dichǎn*, is too deferential, and *chǎn* is not deferential enough. Another term, *nǔu*, is too childish, and use of her own name or nickname (which can generally be used pronominally), may appear too informal or intimate in this situation. It may be that there is simply no way to refer to herself that is completely acceptable, and the young woman might attempt to avoid using any first person form at all—obviously not an easy matter. Just try carrying on a conversation of any length some time without saying "I."

Missionaries trying to translate the Bible into Thai ran into a similar problem in selecting the appropriate forms to use in connection with Jesus. To use extremely high or deferential forms elevated Him too far above ordinary people. Yet to use plain language tended to be disrespectful and to deny His divinity. Finally, they were forced to use the higher language and then find a way to reduce it so as to indicate His humanity.

In addition to the royal aristocracy and high-ranking government officials, other positions of considerable status in Thailand include priests, doctors, professors, and teachers. Highly educated persons in general are treated with much greater deference in Thailand than is common in the U.S. Private business has traditionally been shunned, at least in part, by the Thais because it offered no titles and positions of power comparable to those which were conferred on government officials as "servants of the king." There are indications, however, that the traditional appeal of government service as a career is weakening and that careers in private business are becoming correspondingly more attractive. This development is reflected in the dramatic increase over the last twenty years in the number of Thais studying business.

Manifestation of status among Americans is considerably more subtle since there exists neither a clear-cut hierarchy nor the accompanying signs of respect and deferential language which characterize status in Thailand. Grounded in the notion expressed earlier that an American must carve out his or her own niche is the corollary that one must earn or achieve status. Thus, an American's status is determined primarily by occupation and earnings. Professionals whose occupations require a high level of academic training or who are financially well rewarded (doctors, lawyers, scientists, business executives) are thus accorded high status. At the same time, achievement itself confers status even if it did not produce wealth. As one moves down the ladder, questions of status blur since many white-collar, professional positions pay less than blue-collar, mechanical jobs. Thus, in many instances, it is difficult to tell who has more status—a school teacher, a construction worker, an electrician or a bank clerk. Further complicating the question of status in the U.S. is its egalitarian ethos.

It is not easy for a high-ranking Thai to feel quickly at home in the more egalitarian American social order. The accustomed demonstrations of respect and deference are not forthcoming, and informal leveling expressions such as "buddy," "Mac," "lady," appear crude and demeaning, as does the American penchant for using first names immediately upon being introduced. Thais must come to understand that this is also the way that Americans, particularly those in service occupations, address their fellow citizens. Thus, although such conduct might be considered impolite in Thai terms, it is the accepted norm in the U.S.

Most Americans are accorded fairly high status in Thailand, particularly well-educated professionals and business managers. While this high status is initially flattering, Americans experience some difficulties in blending smoothly into the social hierarchy. Alex de Tocqueville, writing in the 1830s, perceptively noted the problems that an egalitarian-minded American has in finding a place when suddenly thrust into a highly stratified society:

> He is afraid of ranking himself too high; still more is he afraid of being ranked too low. This twofold peril keeps his mind constantly on the stretch and embarrasses all he says and does.... His house will be in the most fashionable part of the town; he will always be surrounded by a host of servants.

Thais are thus sometimes amused at the speed with which Americans in Thailand are able to shed their egalitarian mantle and surround themselves with the trappings of success—such as having a car and driver and a maid—soon living in a manner to which they were formerly unaccustomed.

While Americans can appreciate the value of having a high status in Thailand, it can also be unnerving. One American company director went to the cremation of a staff member's father. At the cremation it was raining, and the Thais insisted on giving the one and only available umbrella to the top executive. Further, they insisted on his sitting in the only chair, and then, to show deference, they sat on the ground in a lower position. "This made me very uncomfortable," he said, "but I know they felt very pleased that the boss came to the cremation."

By contrast, a senior Thai official remarked that he did not enjoy his holiday at a particular U.S. resort, where hotel staff mixed freely on a social basis with guests. He preferred the more traditional hotel in Thailand where guests are treated with deference.

Considerable patience and understanding on the part of both Thais and Americans is clearly called for here. Americans must try to get some sense of the harsh leveling which a Thai experiences on entering the U.S. Similarly, Thais should realize that Americans new to Thailand sometimes find it difficult to understand their role in the Thai hierarchical system. For example, the head of a U.S. corporation was unsure about whether or not to use the deferential word *krap* at the end of his sentences when speaking to subordinates. The advice he received did not help a great deal. He was advised by one person to use the deferential term to convey his "fatherly" concern for his subordinates and by another person to hold himself above others since he held the highest position in the company and not use *krap* at the end of his sentences. It takes some time to develop a sense of when situations require use of the deferential term and when they do not.

Expression of Emotion

When comparing the more assertive way Americans express their individualism with the generally nonassertive manner in which Thais manifest theirs, we noted that one of the ways this difference was reflected was in the manner in which emotion is expressed. The direct, forceful American style stands out in sharp contrast to the subtle, indirect pattern in Thailand.

Consistent with the Buddhist ideal that ultimate happiness (nirvana) results from the total detachment of the self from feelings and desires, Thai emotional expression—whether it be positive or negative—is rarely extreme. Instead, Thais have a tendency to neutralize all emotions; even in a very happy moment, there is always the underlying feeling: I don't want to be too happy now or I might be correspondingly sad later; too much laughter today may lead to too many tears tomorrow.

Thus, even positive emotions are kept under control, helping to reduce the discrepancy between the height of present happiness and the depth of the possible forthcoming sadness. Since Americans generally do not keep such a tight rein on positive emotion, their highs are somewhat higher, and their lows may be correspondingly lower. Indeed, Americans frequently contrast emotional states in everyday speech when they refer to "ups and downs," "highs and lows," emotional "peaks and valleys."[2]

Thais speak approvingly of the one who has *cai yen* (literally, cool heart), or the capacity to restrain emotions and keep interpersonal relations on a smooth, even keel. One should be friendly, pleasant, and polite with other people—not too involved, yet not too distant. In interpersonal relationships, as in all areas of life, a Buddhist sense of moderation is the ideal. Conversely, one who has *cai ráwn* (hot heart) is looked at in a negative light since that person is overly impulsive, impatient, and quick-tempered.

This preference for the cool heart and subdued equanimity is illustrated in the Thai reaction to a visit by a famous movie star. Before landing at the Bangkok airport, some members of the star's party were worried that he might be mobbed by overzealous fans as had happened in other countries. But they needn't have worried, for as the star strode from the plane, no one tore the shirt off his back, no one yelled and screamed; in fact hardly anyone even showed up. Not that the star's films are unpopular in Thailand, for in fact they are box office smashes. It's just that wild adulation of the type often accorded movie stars elsewhere would be totally out of character in a land where a premium is placed on keeping your emotional cool.

An old Siamese tale concerns the violent quarrel which was triggered by a single drop of honey that fell to earth. A lizard crept up to lick it and was attacked by a cat, which was in turn bitten by a dog. Soon the owners of the cat and dog were embroiled in a heated argument which eventually turned into an all-out battle as friends and neighbors rushed to enter the fray. The moral is clear: anger, like a forest fire, must be stamped out at once, before it has the chance to spread and become a calamity of the direst kind.

When Thais perceive that an argument is imminent, an attempt will often be made by one of the persons involved (or by some other person if it is a group situation) to dilute the emotionally charged atmosphere by jokes or a change of topic. Or feelings of anger may be directed elsewhere with the intent of sending an indirect signal to the real target of the anger. For example, an adult might verbally criticize a child or dog while, in actuality, the criticism is meant for another adult who is standing nearby and who is fully aware to whom the words apply.

In general, one should interact with others politely no matter how much anger or annoyance one might feel or, as the Thai saying goes, "Keep muddy waters inside while you put clear water outside." Americans tend to handle anger in the opposite manner, believing that it is better not to "bottle up" one's anger but rather to "let it all hang out." Bringing the anger out into the open has, to the American way of thinking, a cathartic effect, and thus, Americans will sometimes speak of the relief felt after a "good quarrel."

Thais feel that this direct, explosive approach is recklessly playing with the drop of honey; they instead look for ways to nip anger in the bud and will at times go to rather extreme measures to insure that no injury results from an action taken in anger. An ancient law, for example, provided that "when the king calls for his sword in anger, the royal page in attendance shall not hand it over, on pain of death."

One American working in a Thai organization observed that while his Thai colleagues appeared to have good relations and avoid outright conflict, they found subtle ways to get back at one another when angered. One Thai department head became angry when a colleague spoke out against him at a professional meeting. Rather than deal with it immediately in a frank and open discussion, he wrote a critical letter about his colleague to the man's supervisor.

Since this key Thai trait, avoidance of open conflict, can sometimes do more harm than good in a work setting, one American company, as part of the management training program, teaches its Thai staff to use creative conflict resolution techniques. Trainees are taught that conflict is not bad, but can be a stimulus to the development and improvement of the business if handled in a positive way.

Since Thais generally avoid displays of anger as well as overt disagreement of any kind, they develop a high degree of sensitivity in picking up indirect cues to the feelings and emotions of others. This trait is embodied in the concept of *kreng cai*, which involves the desire to be self-effacing, respectful, and extremely considerate as well as the wish to avoid embarrassing others or intruding or imposing on them. Kreng cai seeks to insure that in direct interpersonal relations no one is placed in a position of embarrassment or shame, no one loses face.

Based as it is on intuition and unspoken cues, kreng cai can sometimes lead to communication problems between Thais and Americans, since the latter depend more on verbal signals to get messages across. For instance, a Thai, seeking to be considerate, may not ask about something that is unclear or bring up a problem with an American colleague, expecting that the American will deduce that something is the matter. Since the American hears no specific verbal complaint, he or she has no reason to suspect that anything is wrong. The Thai may then go away upset, feeling that the American is insensitive; the American, from a different perspective, has no way of knowing that a problem has arisen, never having been told explicitly.

Though equanimity and diffusion of anger is the Thai goal, in practice such disciplined control is not always possible, as in the student-led revolution of 1973 which toppled the government and drove three high-ranking officials into exile. Tension had reached such a peak that violence was inevitable given the students' steadfastness and the government's intransigence. But when the outburst was over, the students quietly restored order to Bangkok, then just as quietly returned to their role as students under the authority of their teachers and the king.

The very fact that such aggressive, outspoken activism caught so many by surprise shows clearly how it contrasted sharply with the traditional pattern. And notwithstanding this unusual, indeed unprecedented, massive demonstration, the fact remains that interpersonal relationships are generally still characterized by harmony rather than rancor, by consideration rather than conflict.

Proper Versus Accurate

Paralleling the Thai pattern of controlled, restrained emotional expression is a corresponding concern with the appropriateness of a wide range of conduct—from body movements to clothing styles, from public displays of affection to the public airing of controversial, discomforting issues. In all of these areas the Thais have a finely honed sense of what is proper, suitable, or màw. Generally, something is màw if it is pleasing to the eye or ear, fits in smoothly with its physical or verbal environment, and leads to congruence rather than dissonance. But Thais need not concern themselves with such a precise, analytical description; something is either màw or it isn't. You know it or you don't—and most Thais do.

On the other hand, if something is totally unsuitable, Thais might say that it doesn't *khâw thâa*, or doesn't even begin to conform to the accepted norm. Although the word *thâa* is used in several different contexts, it generally refers to a posture, a position, or a picture. It is almost as if Thais had a mental picture or image of exactly what a particular scene should look like, and if something doesn't fit in, it doesn't khâw thâa or literally doesn't enter into the picture.

This whole approach deals mainly with the form or appearance of things, for to Thais form is of crucial importance. Americans, on the other hand, do not share the Thais' scrupulous concern with the way things look. They are more concerned with the way things are. They speak of cutting through the appearance to get at the reality, the truth of the matter. What is important is not form but substance, not outer show but inner content. This is reflected in such sayings as "honesty is the best policy," or more recently, "tell it like it is." Never mind if someone's feelings are bruised in an honest appraisal of the situation, for we are concerned with the higher goal of truth; that is the way Americans tend to look at things.

Particularly important to Americans is getting beyond the polite facade or even unmasking hypocrisy if necessary in order to reveal who the person or what the situation really is (after all, honesty is the best policy). And because Americans have set their ideals so high (as embodied in the Declaration of Independence, the Constitution, etc.) and have promised themselves so much, they can usually find a discrepancy between the loftiness of the ideals and the less noble social reality they see around them. Thus, Americans are extremely (some would say morbidly) self-critical, and social critics from Thoreau to Philip Slater have written about the weaknesses of American society with an unrelenting bitterness which Thais (and others) find difficult to comprehend.

One American professor working in a Thai university recalls being very frustrated when he and a Thai colleague hosted a visiting delegation from another university abroad: "In explaining our department's program, my colleague painted our situation in rosy terms and showed our visitors a handsomely printed university catalog that listed lots of courses which we never give. I felt we should have had a frank and open dialogue, spelling out some of our problems so that we could all learn from the exchange."

Thais, on the other hand, are going to be less likely to hang out their dirty laundry in public. When a Thai has a problem, he or she might describe 20 percent of it to others, leaving 80 percent to be guessed at or assumed. An American would be more likely to spell out the whole 100 percent. For example, when a supervisor asks a Thai staff member to do a job which the staffer is unable to fulfill, the staffer might give a vague answer like, "I'll try to do it if I finish this other assignment," rather than coming out with a straight "no." Americans working in Thailand gradually begin to understand the subtle messages their Thai colleagues are giving them, just as Thais living in the U.S. gradually learn that an American's blunt answer does not convey hostility or intentional offense. Honesty, to Thais, may not always be the best policy, and they would tend to agree with Shakespeare that "though it be honest, it is never good to bring bad news." If they have to choose between politeness and honesty, they will usually choose the former, leading one American anthropologist to term Thai politeness a "social cosmetic" in that it at once enhances a person's natural qualities but also inevitably conceals them. The most important aspect, then, of social relationships is the psychological comfort and welfare of the persons involved rather than the objective truth or validity of the matter discussed.

At least a few Thais (especially those familiar with the American concern with hypocrisy) recognize that there is an inherent element of hypocrisy embodied in the Thai approach and tend to view it somewhat negatively. However, most Thais would probably not view this inconsistency between word and thought (if indeed they viewed it as inconsistency at all) as anything particularly deplorable unless it were used for clearly deceitful purpose or personal gain. On the other hand, if a "little white lie" is told merely out of politeness so as not to disappoint or hurt another person, most Thais would probably consider this preferable to critical, "honest," discomforting comments.

This Thai emphasis on politeness or appropriateness of behavior is seen also in their careful attention to controlled, respectful body movements and neat, orderly dress. Since the head is considered the highest part of the body (in a spiritual sense) and the feet the lowest, Thais are far more concerned than Americans about the position of the head and feet and postures in sitting and walking.

One must be careful to avoid touching another's head or having the foot pointed at the head. A subordinate (in age or status) should not place his or her head above that of a superior. The head and sometimes the entire upper body must be bowed if the superior is seated. When walking past another person, whether that person is standing or sitting, one must either walk behind the person or bow while passing in front. When seated, one must take care in crossing the legs to make sure that the toe is not pointed at another person.

Dress should also be somewhat subdued. Extremely informal styles, loud colors, and suggestive, revealing attire are generally avoided; instead, one should look *riâb róy* (neat and orderly). School and university students wear prim, neat, blue and white uniforms and rarely have the bedraggled look of American high school students. Thai women are often quite modest about appearing in a bathing suit, particularly a bikini. One notable exception to this is Thailand's legendary bar girls who bump and grind in the most revealing outfits and walk down the street in tight pants, holding hands with foreign tourists. While many Thais accept such behavior from a prostitute (and Thai men patronize them regularly), sexually explicit dress and behavior in public is not the norm in Thai society.

Americans have no comparable concern for "appropriate" body movements, and though they are certainly not unconcerned with clothing styles, they don't place the same emphasis on a neat, conservative look. In fact, stressing substance rather than form, Americans tend to regard clothing and posture as somewhat superficial matters; the important thing to them is the person's underlying character and competence. Thais, on the other hand, tend to view a person's physical appearance and bearing as indicative of his or her moral nature or character. From an early age Thai children are taught proper postures and movements since society will judge them to a certain extent on the way they handle their bodies.

The failure of Americans to understand the Thai preoccupation with public propriety (or blatant refusal to conform to it if they did understand) generated considerable ill will during the days of the large-scale American military presence. The public displays of affection between G.I.s and Thai women clashed strongly with Thai ideas of proper behavior. Herbert Phillips captured the core of the problem in these words:

> [The] Thai concern about the sexual behavior of American G.I.s and Thai women has to do with the public exhibition of intimacy, not with the private sexual behavior of these persons. Thailand is one of the most sexually relaxed places on earth. But Thais expect people to take their relaxation privately, not to proclaim it on public streets.

In Thailand, then, the question is whether something is fitting, suitable, or proper. The corresponding American concern is whether it is honest, correct, or accurate. If they are to understand one another and work together effectively, both Thais and Americans must accommodate themselves to one another's ground rules. A satisfactory compromise might be one in which each could speak frankly to the other but with a clear understanding that the way in which something is discussed is also of prime importance—a sensitive openness rather than direct, cards-on-the-table American candor or indirect, leave-one-in-the-dark Thai politeness.

Friendship

Americans contrast a "fair-weather friend" with a friend who is "tried and true." Thais draw a similar distinction between "eating friends" and "friends to the death." Eating friends, like fair-weather friends, feast with you when you can feast and swiftly disappear if you fall upon hard times. In certain respects Thai friendship patterns closely parallel American practices, but there are a number of differences as well.

Since both peoples, as noted earlier, prize a somewhat independent existence, their relationships usually do not involve the deep reciprocal set of rights and duties that are characteristic of friendships in more communal societies. The average American, for example, can expect to move fourteen times in his lifetime. Thus, a certain superficial friendliness is a definite asset since it is important to be able to meet people quickly in a new environment. Deep relationships, on the other hand, don't easily stand the strain of continual uprooting occasioned by the mobility of American life.

This is not to say that Americans and Thais do not make good, sincere friends. It's just that the expectations and preferences brought to their relationships are characterized by congenial informality rather than binding reciprocal commitments. In fact, both Thais and Americans will often not call on their friends for help precisely because they are friends. An American, preferring not to inconvenience friends, may seek out professional, impersonal assistance instead. Similarly, because of their concept of kreng cai, Thais are often reluctant to impose on their friends, at least for rather routine favors. One Thai explained that they are taught not to ask, but to give to those who ask; to be self-sufficient and never impose on others, but to be kind and ready to help at all times.

In times of real need, however, Thais and Americans both want to be able to call on their friends. Thus, they stress that above all else a friend must be reliable, a tried-and-true friend, or a friend to the death. Particularly important in this regard is the notion that a true friend will give honest, considered advice, which may involve critical or negative comments if the situation warrants. An American might tell a friend a painful truth, not to hurt but in a sincere effort to help. A Thai will also speak to a friend in a frank and, if need be, critical manner in order to render assistance. This is one of the few instances in which a Thai is expected to be absolutely candid.

One way in which American friendships differ from those of Thais is that Americans tend to be more compartmentalized, centering around an activity, an event, or shared history. A person can have one friend to play bridge with, another to discuss politics with, and a third to go to parties with. This pattern comes about in part because of an American tendency to define people according to what they participate in or have achieved. Americans can deal with the human personality in fragments, viewing the other person (and oneself) as a composite of distinct accomplishments and interests.

Looked at in this way, the other person need not be accepted as a total being to enable interaction; for instance, one may disapprove of the politics, hobbies, or personal life of an associate and yet still be able to work with him or her effectively. Thais, on the other hand, tend to react more to the totality of other individuals and are less inclined to form friendships with someone whose preferences (in many areas of life) they don't approve of.

Another difference in Thai-American relationships concerns what happens when disagreement leads to argument and a previously compatible relationship starts to go on the rocks. In the first place, the likelihood of such an occurrence in Thailand is considerably lessened by the pains that people take to diffuse anger at its inception (remember the drop of honey!). But precisely because a Thai's chances of being personally affronted are so small, his capacity to detect such an affront is finely honed—the sharpest knife nicks the easiest. Since overt arguments are taken so seriously, a verbal fight between two Thais usually ends with each becoming the other's enemy, and they may never be able to resume a friendly relationship. They can, at best, be civil to one another.

Americans have more of a tendency to try to "make up," even after a bitter quarrel; they prefer to "forgive and forget," "kiss and make up," and generally try to restore the relationship to its previous amicable state. This, of course, is not always possible, but it is at least a perceived alternative to unremitting hostility.

Humor and Laughter

Thais in general enjoy a party where there is lighthearted good fun and group amusement. Singing, games, and lots of food and drink are important. Intellectual conversation and one-on-one discussion is not as appealing. The American cocktail party isn't considered particularly enjoyable because it is too "up tight," and there isn't enough food and fun.

As befits their shrewd, astute pragmatism and corresponding disdain for pomposity and arrogance, both Thais and Americans can appreciate subtle, and sometimes earthy humor and clever plays on words. In the U.S. this often takes the form of puns, and Americans skilled in the art can "puntificate" in such rapid-fire fashion that only fellow punsters will be able to follow the more subtle offerings. Thais have a comparable type of word game in which they exchange vowels or consonants between two words. Double entendre and vulgarity are often expressed in this way— the first person will make a statement that sounds completely innocuous, but both the speaker and the listener will silently invert it to arrive at a double meaning.

Unfortunately, most Americans are unable to share this type of humor with their Thai associates since few Americans speak Thai fluently enough to catch the humorous references. Furthermore, although many Americans can speak some Thai, very few can read it well and therefore do not have the same pool of references as Thai colleagues who read Thai newspapers and magazines.

Thais, particularly villagers, also make extensive use of giggles as an important communicative device. One wishing to ask for a favor from a neighbor can use the giggle to hedge around and precede the direct request. Likewise, the one whose aid is being sought can avoid the request simply by giggling; the giggle is merely the polite substitute for "no," or "let's end this particular topic of conversation."

Not without reason is Thailand known as the "Land of Smiles," for the generally happy, friendly demeanor of the people reflects both a basic contentment or joie de vivre as well as a hǎrd-to-dispute conviction that interpersonal relations flow more smoothly when entered into with a smile. What often confuses Americans is that Thais will sometimes smile or laugh in situations which appear to be sad or even tragic, for instance at an accident or funeral. Since Americans are more likely to maintain a sober or grim countenance on such occasions, they are somewhat taken aback to see Thais smile, when to American thinking it is a time for sorrow rather than joy.

Even at funerals Thais will try to put on at least a smiling, if not a happy, face. Again, it is precisely because they feel the loss so keenly that they do not want to dwell on it; they truly laugh so that they will not weep. In the past, plays were put on at funerals, and a good deal of joviality in the form of feasting and playing games still accompanies this most somber event. Whether to express joy, indicate contentment, or banish sorrow, the smile in Thailand literally covers a multitude of emotions.

Mutual Perceptions

Americans have long been well received in Thailand, dating from the mid nineteenth century when American missionaries introduced the printing press and pioneered the development of medical treatment along Western lines. As recently as the beginning of this century, 113 of the 125 Americans in Thailand were engaged in missionary work.

This positive first impression was reinforced by what the Thais perceived as a less condescending attitude by the Americans than that of the Europeans who were there. Thai leaders at the turn of the century looked to Americans as "the nationality of the future" and felt secure to call on them for help in the development of their country.

Prince Desawongse, the Thai foreign minister for thirty-eight years, once confided that Thailand turned to the U.S. rather than to European countries because they saw no danger from American annexation. Accordingly, from 1903 to 1917, three Americans successively held the lofty position of general advisor to His Majesty's government. It is important to note that the employment of these high-level advisors was a voluntary decision on the part of the Thai government; no pressure was exerted by the U.S. government to bring about their appointment.

Thai attitudes toward Western culture generally and things American specifically have been largely favorable, though the overall feeling could perhaps be best termed as one of admiration tinged with ambivalence. Thais, for example, have freely accepted modern medical practices, modern systems of education, and Western consumer goods which make for household comfort. Western religious concepts and teachings, on the other hand, have been consistently rejected or ignored by all classes of society. Missionaries have been tolerated and even welcomed, but it has generally been their contributions in medicine and education, rather than their religious messages, which have been appreciated and emulated.

To put all of this in perspective, it has been primarily middle- and upper-class Bangkokians who have been most interested in Western ways, generally believing that the more Westernized they become, the higher status they are likely to have. This high regard for things Western is reflected in the use of the Thai word *săkon* as a translation for "Western" in such phrases as Western dress and Western motion pictures, for săkon actually means "universal."

In terms of knowledge about and influence of the Western world, again a sharp distinction must be drawn between well-traveled, often Western-educated Bangkokians and their rural counterparts. Because the former are the political, business, and intellectual leaders and the ones that Americans based in Bangkok have most contact with, one can be misled into believing that Thais in general are quite knowledgeable about Western ideas and practices. Actually, the vast majority of Thais outside the big cities know very little about and are little influenced by Western values and customs, apart from what is learned in superficial glimpses of American life in an occasional movie.

As for American perceptions of Thailand, one highly successful Broadway musical and subsequent film—*The King and I*— so distorted the Thai way of life that serious Thai scholars and public relations specialists have not yet succeeded in totally dispelling the myth of the mercurial monarch held spellbound by the self-righteous Victorian school mistress. The movie has long been banned in Thailand because it is considered insulting to a well-respected king. That particular Thai king (Rama IV, better known as King Mongkut) spent twenty-seven years in a Buddhist monastery, was a learned philosopher and theologian, studied Latin and English, was deeply interested in science, and skillfully succeeded in bringing things Western into the realm without sacrificing Thailand's sovereignty.

Unfortunately, the image that many Americans have of this wise, scholarly statesman is one of Yul Brynner bounding adolescent-like about the stage, using body movements and modes of expression that would be unthinkable for a self-respecting Thai farmer, let alone the king.

On a more personal level, Thais and Americans generally interact in a rather congenial way. They share just enough similar qualities—they are both independent, practical, down-to-earth, and well-intentioned, for example—to be able to develop a gut-level understanding of one another. Starting from this commonality, they are then intrigued and at times annoyed by some of their differences. In fact, each can appear naive and somewhat childlike to the other, which, while at times exasperating, can also be charming. Thais sometimes contrast Americans with other *farang* (a term used to refer to all Westerners), whom they view as somewhat mirthless and aloof. Americans are friendlier, ever so earnest, and possess seemingly boundless energy as they tend to their self-appointed tasks in a relentless, bull-in-the-china-shop, but nonetheless amiable, manner.

Like a windup toy run amok, the American can't seem to stop

or even slow down. Why, Thais wonder, must they ask so many specific questions, worry so about time and deadlines, and put so much emphasis on changing things? But the Thais are more curious than annoyed.

Americans also see Thais as genuinely friendly and solicitous to a fault, the most gracious hosts one could imagine. But why, Americans ask themselves, don't they have more self-discipline? If they had more of a sense of responsibility, we could work together much more effectively and productively.

These differences in pace and perspective can occasionally lead to friction, but it is born more out of frustration than anger or dislike. As they learn to work together, Americans and Thais can hopefully adjust to each other better so that, in a practical fashion, a middle road can be found on which they can continue to travel amicably together.

[2]It is useful to remember that any given value, behavior, or other cultural characteristic lies on a spectrum of such characteristics and that the whole spectrum is represented in the world's cultures. How that characteristic is manifest or perceived in any particular culture may be relative to the culture against which it is being contrasted. For instance, Americans may seem to let their emotions go more than Thais do; but in contrast to Latins and Arabs, Americans are generally considered quite emotionally inexpressive. "Cold fish" and "emotionally dead" are two of the stronger expressions used occasionally by Latins and Arabs to describe Americans.

5

Attitudes Toward Work

Work and Play

The idea that work per se is morally good and that there is a direct relationship between hard work and success—the cornerstone of what came to be known as the Puritan, the Protestant, or simply, the work ethic—has left an indelible imprint on the American psyche. Since the ethic endures today, long after the passing of the Puritan colonists, and has in its grip Catholic and Jewish Americans as well as Protestants, it will be referred to here as simply the work ethic. By whatever name, the ethic taught (and experience seemed to bear out) that hard work had its rewards in the U.S. The American worker gained a reputation for immense productivity based on discipline, determination, and long hours of unremitting toil.

Though there is talk now of a changing work ethic in the sense that many workers appear more concerned with security, job satisfaction, shorter work weeks, and a generally looser rein while on the job, the fact remains that most Americans still look with disfavor on the idle person, the loafer, the one who wastes time on anything but a steady job. Time for work has traditionally been viewed as separate from time for recreation or fun. Work is what one does to earn a living. It is supposed to be satisfying in itself. Physical labor is a positive value in the American lexicon and work provides the framework in which one pursues achievements. It is not necessarily supposed to be fun, that is, pursued as play, nor is it to be confused with leisure, which is something that provides relief from the pressures and constrictions of work. Life to the American, then, is essentially compartmentalized. There is a time for hard, hopefully satisfying, but not necessarily enjoyable, work followed by time for relaxation. Americans even speak of a person's social life as if it were a separate life from the life lived on the job.

Thais do not look at work or life in this way. The lofty place that work occupies in the mental priority list of most Americans would be substituted by most Thais with *sanùke* (fun, enjoyment, having a good time). Just as Americans tend to view work per se as a good thing, so Thais generally regard sanùke per se as a good thing. This seems almost heretical to the average American, raised in a culture where play is viewed as an escape from reality and having fun is seen as a normal, necessary, but temporary retreat from adult responsibility.

From the Thai standpoint, however, if something is not sanùke, it is scarcely worth doing. Unlike the compartmentalized approach of Americans, Thais have more of an expectation that all of their activities will be suffused with sanùke. Work, study, and even religious services must have at least an element of sanùke if they are to absorb a Thai's interest; in fact, one of the reasons why there have been so few Thai converts to Christianity has undoubtedly been the failure of the missionaries to make their religion appear more sanùke.

Thais particularly enjoy sanùke activities which are novel and diverting. In the past there was a tendency to plunge energetically into new activities, tasks or projects which were fun, but then to lose interest when the novelty wore off, leaving the project unfinished. This is less true today when both city dwellers and farmers work long and hard at tasks which further the economic development of their country. Nevertheless, Thais still like to punctuate their work or introduce into it, more frequently than

Americans, activities that are designed purely for the enjoyment they provide, transforming the task from work to fun.

One representative of an American foundation which supports Thai projects noted that often he calls on Thai organizations and government offices to explain the work of his foundation. He is frequently asked by Thais why he does this kind of work. "I go into a serious discussion about objectives, etc.," says the American, "but then I tell them I do this kind of work because I like it, because it's sanùke, and they understand right away."

Western-trained Thai technocrats might demur to the above characterization of what might be termed the "traditional" (predominantly rural) Thai approach to work and fun. Schooled in the rigors of modern business practices, they may have internalized Western values to such an extent that they can rightly say that their approach more closely parallels the American model than it does the traditional Thai pattern.

Change

Change may well be the only constant in American society. Lacking deep-rooted traditions, Americans feel comfortable with change, thrive on change, and almost feel that it is a civic, if not moral, duty to bring change about more or less continuously. This attitude of necessity implies a certain dissatisfaction with things as they are, for if one were content with the status quo, there would obviously be no need to change it. Like the work ethic, this notion of change stems in part from the Puritan view that evil which exists in the world must be rooted out.

Americans have thus long felt a sense of mission not only to renew and perfect their own society but also to serve as a model for all mankind. Originally this took the more passive form of the Puritan "City on a Hill" (American society), whose exemplary light was to shine out for all to see. Over the course of the nation's history, the sense of mission took on a more active character as Americans, not content simply to light up their own hill, felt compelled to transport the light overseas so that none could miss it. Though no doubt based on good intentions, this attempt to impose their perspectives on others led to charges that the United States was attempting to impose its way of life on the rest of the world.

Though secular in nature, such enterprises as foreign aid, the Peace Corps, and numerous other American institutions of diplomacy and foreign relations are deeply rooted in the idea that the United States has a special mission in the world. The impact of this more generalized, secular missionary zeal, whose message is simply "the American way," has been far greater than that of the original religious doctrine from which it sprang.

Embodied in the whole notion is the idea that human beings must improve their lot by instigating change; this in turn conforms to the American view of nature described earlier, in which humans are the masters of their environment and can alter it to suit their needs. Americans speak highly of "change agents" working to bring about meaningful change, clearly indicating that it is up to the individual to take an active role in modifying the status quo. Consequently, Americans tend to look despairingly and somewhat patronizingly on more traditional societies (often referring to them as "hidebound"), which seem either unwilling or unable to change.

Like Americans, Thais do believe in change, but they have never felt the same compulsion as Americans to bring it about. Their concept of change and a person's role in it differ in a fundamental way from the American view. For in the Buddhist sense, change is the most certain thing of all; it is what existence is all about—constant cycles of *ùbàt* (birth, beginning, springing up) and *wíbàt* (death, ending, passing away). Since change is so all-pervasive, it would be presumptuous, foolish, and certainly futile for humans to interject themselves in an active way into this process.

The point is that everything is going to change by itself—government, companies, mundane problems are going to come and go. Instead of worrying about how and when these changes are going to occur, it's better to simply keep one's emotions under control, restrain one's concern over life's vicissitudes, and try to develop the wisdom to see how transitory all things really are. Eschewing the American's active approach to change, Thais would agree fervently with Milton: "They also serve who only stand and wait."

This point of view is not congenial to the American mentality, for Americans tend not to look at things in this long-range manner. Based on their experiences, Americans believe that by bringing about change, they can help improve the human condition, at least in a material sense, and that they can do it now. Because they have conquered many formerly deadly diseases, have improved sanitary conditions and medical treatment, and have pioneered the development of numerous beneficial consumer goods, Americans can argue forcefully that more people are living longer and more comfortably than in the past. This is good; let's keep trying to improve things even more.

Thais might counter that no matter how much you change things, no matter how many diseases are wiped out, no matter how pure the water and how clean the air, fundamental facts of existence will remain. Mankind will still suffer, grow old, and die. From the American perspective, this Thai view seems defeatist or at best fatalistic. From the Thai perspective, the American position looks rash and futile.

Who is right? In a sense, both are. It is just that the American view, shaped by the belief that a person has only one go-around on this earth, tends to be more short-range. The Thai idea, influenced by the cyclical Buddhist concept of existence, is much longer-range.

This is not to say that human-initiated change never occurs in Thailand, for in fact throughout its history Thailand has been generally receptive to change. Within the broad, long-range conceptual framework outlined above, there have generally been ruling elites or Western-influenced professionals, who—like Americans—strove to better certain aspects of the status quo. Here it might be said that Thai pragmatism as well as a penchant for present comfort took precedence over the abstract Buddhist doctrine. Thais have thus tended to borrow elements from other societies, modifying them if necessary to fit smoothly into the Thai cultural mosaic.

In recent years there has been considerable change in Thailand. New, modern skyscrapers in Bangkok, like those of the Bangkok Bank, the Thai Farmer's Bank and others, symbolize these changes and indicate that Thailand is adapting to the styles and practices of contemporary international business. One observer comments, "Politically, Thailand has advanced more in the past ten years than any other country in the region. The development of the institution of representative government and the mechanics and channels for the preservation of basic individual freedoms (such as the media and ad hoc protest groups) have all been significant." The Royal Thai government's five-year national development plan charts the course of change and growth in Thailand.

But while significant changes are taking place in Thailand today, Americans and Thais may have different approaches to change in the workplace. One major reason is that change often brings out underlying conflict, which Thais much prefer to avoid. Thais, responding on the basis of deeply ingrained, culturally based attitudes, are much more likely to prefer retaining the status quo than to go through the painful, soul-searching process of identifying problems and placing blame for things that require change. Another major reason for preserving the status quo is the wish to avoid inconveniencing another person with the change and, perhaps, inciting anger and possible retribution.

"People are more important than anything," said one Thai personnel officer whose American company has recently had to lay employees off in response to difficult economic times. "Very seldom would a Thai organization lay a lot of people off. Thais feel that they can't trust American organizations because they don't offer complete job security." On the other hand, Thais consider working for an American company to be good experience. "I like it," said a Thai. "It means there are always new opportunities to achieve new things."

One American businessman in Thailand notes that Thais are willing to accept change in an organization but, like their American counterparts, they like to have the reasons for it spelled out. They also appreciate a chance to give feedback on the proposed change. However, an American boss who says, "Tell me what you think; my door is always open," won't get much response. Some alternative method for seeking reaction must be found, such as nominating one member of the staff to collect comments or requesting that the staff comment through a group memo where no one person is responsible for any opinion expressed.

Thais themselves are not likely to initiate change in a work situation. They are taught by their culture and their educational training, which emphasize rote learning and deference to seniors, not to challenge the system that is in place. But there are ways to get them to participate in organizational development, or the change process. As an experiment, one American executive organized a brainstorming day for all staff and was amazed at the number of sound, creative ideas that came out of it. He had always thought that his Thai staff members, being quiet and reserved, did not think much about the company's operations. He was delighted to find that when encouraged to speak up in a nonthreatening setting, they were full of ideas.

Ambition

Americans have tended to view ambition in a generally positive light; it is something a person should have in order to be successful in life. Underlying this concept of ambition is the assumption that personal achievement is largely a matter of individual determination. One will be rewarded if only one works hard enough. "Where there's a will, there's a way." Americans cite numerous instances of poor children, sometimes unable to speak English, who have risen to great heights as business tycoons, political leaders, scientists, entertainers, or athletes largely because of their own hard work and determination. This notion that one can literally go from "rags to riches," popularized in the Horatio Alger stories, has inspired many an American to put in prodigious amounts of time and effort in an attempt to improve his or her lot in life.

Since achievement obviously requires an all-out effort, Americans place a great emphasis on being active, keeping busy, and above all "doing" something. It is the person who performs visible deeds rather than the contemplative intellectual who is accorded high prestige in American society. Inventors are more praised than poets; doctors of medicine outrank doctors of philosophy. This "doing" orientation in American life is reflected in numerous colloquial expressions: "How're you *doing?*" "What do you *do* for a living?" "What do you want to *do* when you grow up?" One should be active, energetic, and steadfast in pursuit of a distant goal.

The traditional Thai view of ambition has been considerably lower key. Central to the Thai attitude is the idea of *karma*, which might be thought of as the sum total of merit and demerit that a person has inherited from a previous life and the store of rewards and punishments which accordingly must be enjoyed or endured in this life.

There is clearly an element of predestination here, for as one has sown in one's past life, so will one reap in this life. Thai parents consequently tend not to encourage their children to be ambitious or pressure them to achieve. If they are destined to arrive at some position—say, to become prime minister—it will simply happen. This does not mean that a person should be totally passive and fatalistic since appropriate action is called for to ensure a satisfactory position in one's next life. But given the many lifetimes one has in which to work out one's religious destiny, achievement in this life does not loom as large in the total picture of existence as it does for an American who views this life as a single journey.

Since Buddhism teaches that a craving for power and prestige will only bring suffering or unhappiness, one who manifests a strong ambition to attain these goals has traditionally been looked at with disapproval by Thai society, for that person is perceived as being solely interested in worldly goods. This does not mean, however, that Thais don't take advantage of opportunities that present themselves; they would attribute it to a good karma and make the most of it.

Apart from Buddhist undergirding, which has tended to diminish overt manifestations of ambition, the Thai temperament itself, inclined to sanùke more than to striving, has played its part in restraining obsession with achievement. Thus, relatively easy work with adequate pay has generally been preferable to hard work with higher pay. And the best combination of all, from the standpoint of many Thais, would be an easy job and good pay. For hand in hand with a preference for sanùke goes a corresponding desire to be *sabaaj* (comfortable, untroubled).

Many Thais are therefore surprised and not a little amused when Americans either can't get a job because they are overqualified or else take a job for which they are overqualified and then complain that the work isn't challenging enough. Such a solution would seem ideal to many a Thai, since in working at less than full capacity—perhaps one step below their actual ability—Thais would feel more at ease or sabaaj than in a more demanding job where they felt pressured to perform up to their supposed full potential. (Interestingly, if Americans followed this pattern, they would never have to worry about the "Peter Principle," for no one would ever reach his or her own level of incompetence!)

The usual caveat must be added that the above description does not fully apply to Westernized Bangkokians, who tend to share with Americans a preference for a demanding, prestigious position. As one young, enterprising Thai professional pointed out, the Thai expression, "Don't set your ambitions beyond your station," was coined no doubt by some high-ranking noble who clearly had a vested interest in seeing that those below him in the hierarchy adhered to it. But this young professional and other Western-trained Thais want to use the skills they have acquired abroad and appear willing to sacrifice some "sabaaj-ness" to tackle demanding jobs which will allow them to live up to their potential. It will be interesting to see what new pattern may emerge as sanùke and sabaaj link up with the work ethic and Theravada Buddhism tries to accommodate Horatio Alger.

Competition, Motivation and Materialism

Inherent in American concepts of individualism and ambition is a constant struggling or striving to improve one's position or, as we said earlier, to carve out one's niche or station in life. Since achievement is viewed as largely a matter of individual effort and since status is determined chiefly by how successful one is in this individualistic pursuit, the motivating factor of competition is a strong stimulant to goad the American ever upward. For it is through competition that the best rise to the top, and achievement where competition is lacking—whether it be in the political, economic, or athletic realm—is looked on with mingled distrust and disdain by most Americans.

Thus, Americans are generally hostile to one-party or individual rule of any kind. They have set up elaborate antitrust laws to ensure competition in business and pay the ultimate tribute to an athlete by calling that person a good competitor. While this competitive cast to American society is viewed as ruthless by some outsiders, most Americans accept and even thrive in such an atmosphere; even those bested in the competition give at least grudging respect to those who ultimately win out and are stimulated to try that much harder the next time.

Although, as we have commented before, Thais share certain individualistic tendencies with Americans, the hierarchical nature of their social order—based as it is on deference to rank—combined with the generally restrained approach to ambition and achievement have served to preclude competition as a significant motivating force. In addition Buddhism supposedly teaches that craving for wealth and power will only bring unhappiness. What then motivates a Thai to engage in hard work, particularly in the private sector, where, as noted earlier, the titles and prestige associated with government service have been unavailable?

Here we quite simply run into a discrepancy between what one would expect a Thai to do based on a literal reading of Buddhist scripture (i.e., renounce worldly goods) and what is actually happening in contemporary Thai (especially urban) society, where it is difficult to detect any significant deficiency in materialistic drive. This should not be particularly surprising, for a clear parallel could be drawn to American society. If someone who had never been to the United States looked on the Bible as predictive of American behavior, he would no doubt have some trouble if, on coming to the United States, he tried to reconcile the obvious materialism he saw all around him with the Sermon on the Mount.

A Thai may be a Buddhist, but he is also a pragmatist, a realist, and a seeker of present enjoyment rather than other-worldly bliss. While the overall influence of Buddhist thought on Thai society can hardly be overemphasized, it is clear that some of the traditional practices of the religion do not mesh well with a modern, urban, materialistic way of life.

But what would induce a Thai to work for an American company as opposed to a Thai company or the Thai government, where the prestige assumedly would be greater? Given the materialistic strain in Thai society, it should not come as a complete surprise that the chief motivating factor is money, for Thais can earn considerably more working for an American company than they could for either a Thai company or the Thai government. But there are several other important reasons as well. First, they view working with an American company as the best way to learn the latest techniques and procedures in the field. Second, they consider the American management system to be streamlined, efficient, and effective, which has its attractions despite the cross-cultural adjustment that may be called for in working within it. Third, there is usually a good program of overseas training. Fourth, they appreciate the fact that promotion will be forthcoming, if earned, and will not depend on flattering the boss. Additional positive features of working for an American company include modern office facilities (furniture, machines, telephones, etc.), good employee benefits, and the chance to practice English.

It sounds good so far, but there are two serious drawbacks, chief of which is a lack of security. Despite the advantages listed above, there is always the nagging fear that they may be laid off or even fired if market conditions or their performance so warrants. In this respect, American efficiency, which they generally appreciate, appears rather heartless, and they fear the harsh suddenness with which the axe might fall. The other drawback is a belief that some American companies reserve top-level jobs for American expatriate staff—hardly conducive to good employee morale and motivation.

Taking Risks and Failure

Risk-taking on the part of Americans is based on well-established precedent: their forebears gave up everything they had in Europe (which admittedly in many cases wasn't much), gambled their lives on a dangerous ocean voyage, and then often risked everything again by moving from settled communities to face the uncertainties of life on the frontier. "Nothing ventured, nothing gained" became the watchword, and whether it was panning for gold in California, plunging heavily into the stock market, or venturing a final dollar to set up one's own business, the American historically has been willing and even eager to risk it all on one turn of the wheel.

Though the abandon of decades past has to a certain extent given way to an ever increasing concern for financial security—for the steady return rather than the dramatic windfall—simple statistics on mobility and new business start-ups indicate that vast numbers of Americans are still ready to set off for greener pastures at the drop of a well-placed suggestion.

The vastness of the land and the opulence of its resources have reinforced the American's belief that the limits to achievement are found only within the individual. If one tries hard enough, one will ultimately succeed. Failure will generally not be attributed to a lack of resources, the government, fate or other external causes. It will most often be attributed to lack of effort, skill, persistence or whatever on the part of the individual. Success and failure, defined as they are in such intensely personal terms, can lead to considerable ego inflation for those who make it and a corresponding deflation for those who don't.

Thais tend not to view life in such all-or-nothing terms. Traditionally more concerned with comfort and security than all-out individual achievement, Thais have not generally been bold risk-takers. Since government positions offered both comfort and security as well as the coveted titles, Thais have been content to blend smoothly into the benign bureaucracy rather than strain and struggle to get ahead in the competitive business environment.

Apart from its failure to provide titled positions, business has generally not been in tune with the Thai temperament. One outspoken Thai quickly catalogued five reasons why this is so: (1) Thais don't like to take the risks which business requires; (2) Thais are relatively easily satisfied and see no reason to struggle to get more; (3) business involves being under pressure, which is not particularly appealing; and (4) Thais don't like to cheat others (apparently an unfortunate *sine qua non* for doing business in the eyes of many Thais).

Having said this, we should point out that many, many Thais have had successful careers in business—from banking, to real estate, cattle ranching, poultry farming and orchid raising—on a high-powered international scale. Hundreds of Thais study business in the United States, and Thailand's ethnic Chinese citizens contribute a great deal of business expertise to the country. As Thailand develops, so does the size and sophistication of Thailand's businesses.

The Thai word for a person who is a failure (*khon lóm lěw*) conveys considerably less stigma than does the corresponding English word. There is more of a tendency, both on the part of the society and the individual, to attribute that unhappy state to outside forces, such as fate, demerit from a past life, or simple lack of inherited capacity, for which one is in no way at fault. Though from the individual's standpoint there might be an element of human rationalization involved as well, the fact remains that a Thai would probably not go through the same painful introspection as would an American similarly situated.

There are signs, however, that traditional Thai attitudes toward government service and business are changing, perhaps significantly, and that the former is no longer viewed in the wholly positive light it once was. Ambitious, materialistic, and willing to take risks, a growing number of well-educated urban Thais are challenging some long-held cultural values concerning work, comfort and prestige. Call it Western, modern, or simply pragmatic, this drive to achieve will no doubt further the development of Bangkok along the lines of the industrialized West. It may also further widen the gap between residents of the island-like capital and their more traditional up-country kinsmen.

Profile of a Thai in an American Organization

Having examined traditional Thai attitudes toward work, play, ambition, motivation, and risk taking, and having seen the influence of urbanization and Westernization on these values, let us now attempt to draw a composite picture of a Thai man or woman who would be interested in working for an American firm, particularly at the managerial level. Let us also see what expectations and apprehensions he or she might bring to that job and what effect, if any, working for an American firm would have on his or her position in Thai society.

We have already seen that salary would probably be the primary motivating factor but that other aspects of the work situation—efficiency, advancement, training, benefits, etc.—would also be of considerable importance. Thus, a Thai coming to work for an American firm would tend to be somewhat materialistic, interested in upward mobility, eager to learn new techniques and practices (and so much the better if this could be done abroad), and generally somewhat above average in daring and self-confidence in order to cope with the demands of working in an alien cultural environment. Thais repeatedly use the words *klâa* (to be bold, dare) and *chyâ mân nai tua eng* (to believe strongly in oneself) in describing the type of person interested in working for an American firm.

In exchange for the benefits listed above, the prospective employee will be aware that he or she must make some considerable sacrifices as well. The Thai employee must adapt to an intensive, demanding work system. The new Thai employee in an American company may have joined the company because of an admiration for Western business ways but may feel uncomfortable in those ways, particularly in the use of English. Though he or she may realize that speaking up in meetings is valued in a Western organization, it may be difficult at first to be comfortable articulating concepts in a foreign language. Practice, of course, takes the edge off these anxieties.

Naturally, a Thai who has studied for an advanced degree in the U.S. or another English-speaking country will not have the same concern about expressing himself in English, but even this individual may not feel completely at home in the language, particularly in the fast give-and-take atmosphere of a meeting. Thais sometimes feel that in this setting they are at a distinct disadvantage since it is often, they believe, the most persuasively presented idea rather than the most sound proposal that carries the day.

When a Thai starts work for an American firm, he or she expects that the company will operate essentially as it would in the U.S. and hopes (at least to a certain extent) that it will, for one of the reasons the Thai seeks this employment is to learn American procedures and practices. At the same time, the Thai hopes that the Americans employed there will have some understanding of and sensitivity to Thai customs, for after all they are in his homeland.

Adapting to the new work environment will probably pose few serious problems, notwithstanding some of the initial apprehensions, for Thais pride themselves on their ability to *pràb tua ngâi* (adjust easily) to new, unfamiliar situations. Similarly, the Thai will find it relatively easy to merge smoothly back into Thai society when away from the office, that is, there will be no major conflict between the "American approach" followed during the day and the "Thai approach" followed while at home. Only if a Thai starts to act in an exaggeratedly American way in terms of rigid punctuality, outspokenness, etc., would he or she perhaps slightly antagonize some Thais. But this would be a rare case, and even if he or she were to display a few American mannerisms left over from the work world, Thais would scarcely give it a thought.

A Thai man or woman would be quietly proud to be employed by an American firm, for it would show that he or she must be a competent, efficient worker. Though some people might consider such an employee a *samun* (underling, lackey) for working for a foreign firm, most people would tend to look on the position favorably (and perhaps slightly enviously), since they believe that an American company would tend to hire employees who are competent and highly qualified. Actually, many people would not look on it with approval or disapproval but would simply be *cheǒi cheǒi* (somewhat indifferent), completely in line with Thai concepts of individualism and emotional expression discussed earlier. For this is the person's job and own personal affair and nothing for others to get excited about one way or the other.

6

Relations at Work

In the Organization

Americans combine the cultural values we have been discussing in this book into a notion of organization involving the mobilization of resources for purposeful action and achievement. This organizational notion is heavily dependent on the horizontal coordination of different operational units and the identification and utilization of external resources (also horizontal). If such coordination and orchestration are successful, then the project, program or operation will be considered well-organized.

A valued employee in such a system is one who works hard and steadily (so as not to waste the employer's time and money), is constantly looking for ways to improve existing procedures, and is capable of successfully coordinating work with people in other departments if the occasion demands. And if an employee can cut through red tape and devise ways to perform work more efficiently, so much the better.

The traditional Thai pattern reflects a different set of values and priorities, and, not surprisingly, the overall societal emphasis on "vertical respect" relations and submission to authority shows itself again in the area of organizational structure. One Thai expressed the basic pattern quite succinctly: "We always look up." The subordinate is thus above all else concerned with complying with the wishes and orders of the superior, who is in turn "looking up" to the next level of authority, and so on. Bold initiative is generally out of place, for it may tangle the delicately linked chain connecting one slot in the hierarchy to the next.

Assertively challenging the authority of one's superior is out of the question, and the superior, in turn, is generally not interested in soliciting opinions from subordinates since the traditional view has been that the one in authority is free to exercise power without consulting underlings. Even were the boss to give subordinates license to debate and criticize, other cultural factors such as kreng cai and a tendency to mute differences of opinion would tend to preclude a candid exchange.

If the concept of organization in the sense of purposeful integration can be considered the cornerstone of the American system, the corresponding Thai notion might be *pen rabìab* (to be in good sequential order). The American pattern highlights horizontal consolidation; the Thai system, vertical protocol. In order for something to pen rabìab, there must be an unbroken upward flow of documents and approval. Correspondence, reports, purchase orders, and requests of various kinds must all, as the Thais would say, "pass many desks" until they arrive at the ultimate superior.

Adherence to protocol fulfills two important functions. It insures that power and authority will be concentrated in the top person, bearing out the truth of the adage that knowledge is power. For here the chief will, of necessity, know all, or at least be in a position to easily refer to any matter should the need arise. To the Thais, this is of utmost importance. For should someone outside the section or department ask about something for which the chief is responsible, the chief must be able to put his or her finger on it immediately and discuss it intelligently. If the chief cannot do so, the situation will be *pralàad* ("strange," in the sense of being awkward), and that person's whole position as a superior (leader) will be considerably undermined.

The system does more than simply protect the chief, however;

it also protects subordinates. They quite literally pass the buck upward, and the boss must assume complete responsibility for all that transpires in the office. In other words, if the boss were called to task for some failing in the department, it would be most unseemly to pin the blame on one of the subordinates. The chief is the chief; and if there's something wrong, it's the chief's fault.

Thais, in attempting to keep things in good order (pen rabìab) are mainly looking up and down. Americans, in trying to make things well organized are often, if not usually, looking sideways. One Thai businessman who participated in the planning for a big American Fourth of July event in Bangkok was struck by the way all the Americans worked together sorting out responsibility among themselves without a leader delegating jobs. Thais would have needed a designated leader assigning responsibilities.

Managerial specialists from the West have written critically of the traditional Thai system, calling it duplicative, inefficient, and not well organized. But these comments reveal an ethnocentric bias, for they miss the point that the Thai system is extraordinarily well organized (or, perhaps better, well ordered) to fulfill the demands of deep-seated cultural values. What has historically been important to the Thais has not been Western notions of productivity, efficiency, and coordination but rather protocol, deference to rank, respect for authority, and smooth interpersonal relationships.

Seeking Assistance

In discussing Thai and American individualism, we noted that both peoples, prizing their independence and self-reliance, usually look first to themselves to solve their problems. But at times this highly individualistic approach is inadequate, and outside assistance must be sought. This was early recognized in Thai history by King Ram Khamhaeng, who, in the thirteenth century, hung a huge bell from the palace gate, to be tolled by anyone who wanted to discuss a problem personally with the king.

But as the centuries wore on, first the bell and later a drum fell silent as people hesitated to take the initiative to strike them. Only in the mid-nineteenth century did King Mongkut wisely decide to come out of the palace and to seize the initiative in opening the dialogue so that the people would feel more comfortable. In so doing he conformed beautifully to an underlying Thai principle: it is the "side that gives" (the superior) rather than the "side that receives" (the subordinate) which should initiate such a sensitive discussion. It is far less embarrassing for an understanding superior, the one in the position of power and authority, to allude to a problem than it would be for a lowly *luuk náwng* (subordinate).

This has clear implications for American managers, advisors, and educators working with Thais, for in the American setting it is generally the one with a problem who seeks out a counselor rather than the other way around. Indeed, if not told of a problem, the counselor or supervisor generally has no way of knowing that it has arisen since the expectation in the U.S. is that the initiative will come from the one who needs help. An American working in Thailand, however, will have to begin to look for subtle indications that a subordinate may have a problem and then start the ball rolling by bringing it up with the individual in question. Or, conversely, Thais working under an American's supervision will have to be urged to make the first move so that the supervisor will know of their problems. Unless some ground rules are laid down, the Thais may feel that the supervisor or counselor is not particularly understanding; whereas from the supervisor's point of view, no news concerning problems is literally good news. The American may wrongly assume that all is well unless he or she hears to the contrary.

Consideration and Confrontation

The American preference for bringing problems out into the open and discussing them in a frank, candid manner so that "we can see exactly where we stand" contrasts sharply with the Thai tendency to avoid direct confrontation so as to preserve surface harmony. American expressions such as "get it straight from the horse's mouth," "tell it like it is," and "stop beating around the bush" illustrate this inclination to meet problems head-on. Among Thais, however, as we noted earlier, serious and sometimes permanent damage is done to relationships when the stage of open argument is reached. Since face-to-face conflict is not viewed as a satisfactory solution to most problems, in Thailand it may not only be necessary but also desirable to beat around the bush in order to forestall an abrasive, open clash. Such an approach can appear evasive and insincere to the American, whereas the American style can seem harsh and insensitive by Thai standards.

This does not mean that a Thai supervisor will not speak directly to a subordinate concerning problems with the latter's work, for in terms of their slots on the hierarchy, both expect that it may at times be necessary for the chief to set the underling straight. However, great importance is attached to the way in which this is done so that the superior—even though direct and candid or as Thais say *trong pai trong ma* (straight going, straight coming)— strives also to be fair, respectful, and polite.

Personal and Business

A certain business orientation pervades American life as opposed to a more social orientation predominant in Thailand. To an American, life centers around one's job. It is more than simply a means of earning a living; it is the standard by which a person gauges personal success and the barometer by which society measures status. Thus, the American tends to work long and hard and takes pride in doing so. Even in social settings, there is considerable job-related talk as Americans discuss their latest projects, plans and proposals. This seriousness of purpose is carried over into free time, where Americans pursue recreational activities, such as running, with a studiousness and determination similar to the attitudes they bring to work—as in the flood of jogging manuals, marathon clinics, and scientific discourse on the construction of running shoes.

Thais traditionally have not considered work the be-all and

end-all of life and have not shared Americans' zest for business-related conversation outside the office. In fact their pattern is quite the opposite; social talk tends to spill over into the work environment. Not only that, the rhythm of Thai life has allowed for social or personal time within work hours—to chat with friends, make phone calls or run errands. Thus, Thais coming to the United States or going to work for an American company in Thailand (again, Westernized Bangkokians excepted), are often struck by the relentlessness of the work environment, by the notion that one should be *constantly* working. A young Thai woman who worked as a grocery checker in the U.S. said that she felt like a machine; there was not time even to relax, let alone perform personal errands! The incessant American work pattern seemed not to allow for the most basic social amenities.

By American standards, Thai supervisors have traditionally been lenient in allowing time off from work so that employees can attend to extended family problems. Thus, misunderstandings may arise between an American supervisor and Thai employees when time off to handle such matters is requested. From the American perspective, this may seem irresponsible, as if the individual is just trying to get out of doing the job or is inappropriately using company time to take care of personal matters. In terms of Thai customs, the American's approach may seem rigid and unfeeling, a case of misplaced priorities. Again, some compromise appears to be called for to accommodate the views of both cultures.

This very different approach to life was one of the hardest things for an American anthropologist working in Thailand to get used to. Once in the midst of an important interview, his Thai field assistant told him—with no forewarning—that he had to leave because he had to be in Bangkok in an hour and a half. He explained that he had promised a friend he would meet him at the movies and thus had to go. When asked why he had made a movie date during working hours, he answered, "Well, this was the only time my friend could go." Several incidents of this kind with different assistants convinced the American that he and his Thai coworkers were clearly operating on different cultural wavelengths.

With his lineal sense of time, the American had planned and scheduled his work. This was the day to conduct the interview. Tomorrow he would hand out a questionnaire. The next day he would go over the answers, etc. To waste a day, or even worse, several, would violate his deeply ingrained sense of the productive usc of time. He had no doubt received a sizable grant to carry out his research. How could he justify just sitting there enjoying the shade of a coconut palm?

To his Thai assistant, such thinking was clearly bizarre. What difference could it possibly make whether the interview was carried out today, tomorrow, or next week? The villagers are always going to be here; what's the rush? My friend, on the other hand, can only go to the movie *now*; so it's clear I have to go. To the American way of thinking, the Thai approach seems unpredictable and wasteful. In Thai terms, the American pattern precludes spontaneity and takes the fun out of life.

7

Cross-Cultural Dimensions in Business

Organization

The nerve center of the intricate Thai organizational system of protocol is what is called in Thai the *saraban* section. There is really no adequate English equivalent of this term, involving as it does elements of record-keeping, office management, and correspondence flow. Essentially this section is responsible for seeing to it that all documents flow smoothly from subordinates to superiors, that they go from desk to desk to desk until they finally settle gently into the top person's in-box. The saraban section does more, however, than merely perform a messenger service. It also keeps detailed files which record this massive paper flow, so that if one wanted to quickly see the step-by-step progression of a particular matter, it could be done by pulling out the appropriate light blue folder from the saraban cabinet. There must be for every transaction that takes place in the office a *làkthaan* (a basis or foundation) in the form of a written document of some kind, which eventually finds its way to the superior and is replicated in the saraban file.

If a subordinate were to initiate some independent action, such as to write a letter to another firm or agency, without following the step-by-step procedure outlined above, it would be considered a personal matter—outside the scope of his or her department's work. It would not pass the chief's desk for approval; it would be outside the saraban chain, and, for all official purposes, it would be viewed as not having even taken place. This again is rooted in the idea that the superior must know everything about the work of the section so as to avoid the *pralaàd* situation of being asked about something of which he or she has no knowledge.

The saraban section can be viewed as the oil which keeps the protocol machinery running smoothly. If the chief of this section is adroit and conscientious, documents move quickly and the office functions efficiently. Should the chief be less zealous in moving things about, paperwork will back up, and delays will result. The most intricate manifestation of the saraban system is, of course, the ubiquitous government bureaucracy, but the pattern of thought which underlies it—the vertical emphasis on power, respect, and responsibility—is reflected in the way private companies and educational and other institutions are run as well. But the degree of exactitude demanded by the government system is often not present in a private firm, particularly a small one.

Given the strong vertical orientation of such an outlook and system, the idea of reaching out or coordinating with other departments or agencies is not particularly appropriate. Each organizational entity has its own system of protocol with which it is concerned. Cross-linkages with outside departments could severely tangle these chains of protocol, causing the chiefs of the sections involved to lose the tight rein each has on his or her own domain. The intricate progressions from subordinate to superior would obviously become extremely complicated if several parallel entities were involved.

Americans working in Thailand, particularly in the vast government bureaucracy, have often found it difficult to function in a way that they view as efficient and well organized. Because they are looking for ways to integrate and coordinate and to organize

diverse elements, they are continually searching out parallel entities performing similar functions. They might go so far as to
attempt to fashion linkages among these different agencies without following the detailed protocol procedures within their own
office. In fact, at least initially, they scarcely know that such
procedures exist. Thais may complain that the American's work is
not *pen rabìab*, which often comes out in English as "not well
organized." The American is confused because in Western terms it
is extremely well organized, but not in Thai terms. Cutting through
the red tape may instead be cutting the fabric of protocol holding
the department together.

But let's take a deeper look at the organizational structures of the
two societies and try to catch a glimpse, if we can, of the thought
processes underlying the American pattern based on organization
and coordination and the Thai system based on order and protocol.
It is beyond the scope of this book to offer any definitive answers,
so what follows is presented solely in terms of a possible point of
departure for further discussion and clarification.

Running throughout the American pattern seems to be an
emphasis on rather abstract concepts: leadership, management,
organization. Americans speak freely of dynamic leadership, progressive management, superb organization, etc., almost as if these
abstractions had a life of their own. What is important here is that
they often divorce the concept of leadership from the more concrete reality embedded in the term, that is, the leaders themselves.
In Thai, by way of contrast, it is much more difficult, if not
impossible, to talk of an abstraction like leadership in such a way.
If, for example, a sentence like "the leadership is progressive" is
translated into Thai, it ends up sounding strained, an attempt to
capture the idea which is embedded in the English sentence but
which simply doesn't render satisfactorily into Thai. It does not
seem to be a genuinely Thai sentence. Thais instead speak much
more readily of the qualities of the leaders themselves rather than
of the disembodied concept of leadership.

Gordon Redding, a professor of management, relates this

American (or more generally Western) tendency to think in abstractions to practices in the business world:

> Western thinking uses a lot of abstract concepts. It uses a linear logic and thinks of proven causes and effects linking abstracts such as democratic leadership style leading to job satisfaction, leading to productivity, leading to efficiency, and so on. Western organizations are constructed as logical, ordered systems, divided purposefully into functions which are based on abstracts such as marketing, finance, personnel management.

To juxtapose what might be called a Thai thought process against this Western mode of thinking is difficult. However, it might be possible to gain at least some insight into the Thai pattern by comparing it to the Chinese mode of thinking described in these words by Hajime Nakamura:

> The Chinese had a high regard for particulars, and presented content concretely in accordance with their way of thinking.... Their stand-point, which relied upon and clung to sensory qualities, made them especially sensitive to the complex variety of phenomena instead of the laws and abstractly conceived unity of things.

This would seem to at least open the door to an understanding of the Thai pattern, for Thais also seem more naturally to think in terms of particulars, to be especially sensitive to the complexities involved in any specific situation. Indeed their entire hierarchical structure demands this high-level contextual awareness so that they can properly manifest respect and deference. Their pattern of smooth interpersonal relationships, based as it is on acute sensitivity to the feelings of others, further illustrates this capacity to grasp intuitively the emotional intricacies involved in any particular encounter.

There are obvious problems involved in trying to draw an exact parallel between Chinese and Thai patterns, given their many differences. However, when one considers the historical link of the Thais to China, the influence of the Chinese language on Thai, and the considerable presence of ethnic Chinese Thais in the business community, it is certainly conceivable that similarities might be noted at a deep, cultural level. And this would seem to be the case with respect to their tendency to think in concrete, contextual terms more than in the highly abstract terms which characterize Western thinking.

The American approach functions best at the macro level, reaching out to pull together diverse elements, organizing them and integrating them into large-scale organizational entities. The Thai approach is more suited to the micro level, where extreme contextual sensitivity allows the Thai to show proper respect, follow protocol demands, and generally interact in harmonious fashion. Despite the strengths of the American pattern—its rigorous linear logic, its effective linking of abstract concepts, its ability to organize and integrate disparate elements—it also contains an inherent weakness: based on abstraction and generalization, it may be too rigid to deal with the real world of change and uncertainty. It at times can't see the particular trees for the forest of abstraction.

Thais, on the other hand, may not be able to see the forest for the trees. Paying scrupulous attention to the intricacies of each individual setting, they find it harder to stand back and grasp the general, abstract pattern. Thais thus sometimes perceive Americans as insensitive to the complexity of factors involved in a particular incident. For their part, Americans sometimes question the Thais' capacity for organization and effective coordination.

A Thai executive who has had extensive opportunities to work both with Thais and Americans compares the two systems:

> Americans look at broad concepts and will take decisive action, even though they realize that they might sacrifice something. They don't feel the necessity to wait around to choose a solution which is 100 percent perfect. Thais would look at the fine points, details, and interrelationships in order to make a perfect decision. But this approach may be difficult to implement. When Thais look at a solution, they care about what will happen to people. Americans care about the outcome, not the individual person. Americans would be happy to take a decisive action which achieved 90 percent of the objective and not worry about the negative fallout of the other 10 percent. Thais would

spend a lot of time trying to figure out how to avoid the negative 10 percent.

Says an American executive who has regular contact with Thai government officials:

Thais have a deserved reputation for being cautious and careful in examining a problem. That approach to public policy has kept the Thais from making some major mistakes. They aren't moving ahead with the whiz bang approach, but that doesn't mean nothing is happening. It just means that it takes a good deal more time for something to happen.

The organizational structures in the two societies clearly differ. Whether this reflects a deep-seated cognitive difference is at this point in the realm of speculation. At the very least this would seem to be a fertile area for mutual discussion, exploration, and research. In the meantime, Thais and Americans should recognize the strengths and weaknesses of the two systems and try to forge an amalgam which would combine the best aspects of American organizational techniques and Thai contextual sensitivity.

Supervision

A certain paradox characterizes the relationship between supervisor and subordinate in the two societies. The Thai pattern, involving deference, obedience, and submission to authority, tends to be autocratic and, at least superficially, formal. Yet, beneath this seemingly impersonal veneer, considerable emphasis is placed on the quality of the relationship formed between the boss and the subordinate. Rooted again in the traditional idea of benevolent paternalism, the chief has the right to order but also has the duty to protect and assist.

The American relationship, on the other hand, is characterized by an easygoing informality. Superficially at least, there appears to be more of a feeling of rapport than in the Thai setting; the subordinate may joke with and even good-naturedly "rib" or tease a superior. Yet, given the more compartmentalized nature of American life, the relationship is essentially a business one and might not extend beyond the close of the workday. The supervisor is concerned primarily with the subordinate's competence and output; the subordinate, with being treated fairly by the supervisor. A friendship may develop from their association, but it does not automatically grow out of their roles as employer and employee.

The Thai relationship tends to be more of a total one, with the boss—by the mere fact of being boss—necessarily more involved in the after-work life of a subordinate, serving, for example, as the host or master of ceremonies at the employee's wedding or assisting with a personal problem. In fact, the use of the terms *boss* and *employee* do not seem wholly appropriate here since in English they refer exclusively to the work setting. The Thais often use the words *nai* (originally "master," though now usually rendered in English as "employer" or "boss") and *lûuk náwng* (literally "child" or "younger," usually rendered in English as "subordinate") to refer to the two positions, indicating a more all-embracing paternalistic relationship than boss and employee.

In describing an ideal supervisor, Thais put considerable emphasis on personal qualities, particularly the capacity for empathizing with subordinates. They say that a supervisor should *rúu cai* (literally "know the heart" in the sense of "to understand") or *rúu nisǎi* (know the habits, characteristics, ways of doing things, preferences) of those supervised. In off-hours, the supervisor should be a friend, elder brother, or respected relative, depending upon the ages involved.

If a lûuk náwng is not performing up to par, the supervisor should try to understand the reason why, assist rather than scold, and treat the subordinate with respect and kindness. At the same time, like a concerned parent, the supervisor can insist on obedience and deference. Thus, Thais say that a good supervisor should have "a whip in one hand and a bag of money in the other," possess authority but also *mêtta* (loving, forgiving kindness), or as one Thai put it simply, "He should be like a teacher and a brother at the same time."

It is also very important to treat employees fairly and not show favoritism. Thai thinking along these lines does not exactly parallel American, however. Though Thais generally disapprove of patently favoring one employee over another, they do not negatively view an occasional bending of a rule to assist someone. Americans might tend to be more strict in this area, that is, they might not allow an employee to do something solely because there is a rule or policy against it. They would be worried that the exception to the rule might create a precedent, forcing them to allow the same exception to anyone else who asks it. Thais, more concerned with present context, might consider that somewhat rigid. They might favor making the exception because of the employee's immediate need, leaving the next case to be decided upon its merits.

Deeply rooted Thai attitudes toward gullibility, responsibility, and emotional expression are apparent in their characterization of poor supervisors. Such individuals too easily believe everything they hear, or as Thais say, they have "a light ear." They are not willing to take the blame for unsatisfactory work in their departments but instead try to shift the blame to their subordinates. They react in an overly emotional way to problems rather than coolly trying to set matters straight and are unduly influenced by fawning, flattering subordinates. Thais are particularly scornful of this latter flaw, saying that a person so influenced is allowing others "to lick his shins and lick his legs."

Any attempt to compare job structure and the actual day-to-day method of supervision of Americans and Thais founders on a definition of terms. Descriptions like "highly structured" jobs or "tight" or "loose" supervision are imprecise since, as we have seen before, the overall rhythm and pattern, both in society generally and in the organizational structure specifically, differ considerably in the Thai and American contexts. Thus, in the sense that Thais readily respond to orders and pay scrupulous attention to the demands of protocol, one might say that there is a certain tightness to the supervision and a corresponding structure to their jobs. But, as we noted earlier, once the order has been carried out and the protocol demands have been met, there is considerable looseness or personal freedom until the next order comes down.

The more consistent pattern for an American worker again falls somewhere between these two extremes—never as tightly supervised with respect to a particular order yet never as loosely supervised so as to allow for nonproductive use of time. Since we have been speaking essentially of the traditional Thai pattern, again a caveat must be added concerning a Westernized, urban Thai enterprise which would in some ways more closely parallel the American pattern just mentioned.

To simplify things, one could hazard the following generalization: a traditional Thai (i.e., one little influenced by Western ways), an urban, Westernized Thai, and an American all want to know, at least in general, what is expected of them. To the traditional Thai this generally means a series of orders. To the Westernized Thai and to the American it means a job description or at least a statement of objectives. Once they know in general what they are supposed to do, all three workers then like some freedom or flexibility as to how they actually perform the work. Given their basic preference for personal independence, none like to have the boss standing over them telling them what to do.

Thais particularly do not like a supervisor who is $c\hat{u}u$ $c\hat{i}i$ (fussy in the sense of always poking them or pestering them to do something). In fact a fear that American supervisors might be too $c\hat{u}u$ $c\hat{i}i$ has undoubtedly kept many Thais from applying for jobs with American companies. One Thai neatly summarized his countrymen's preference in these words: "We like to be told what to do and when to do it but not how to do it—except in the training stage." Another said, "I don't like to be pinned down. Give me broad guidelines, and then let me do the job myself."

Both Americans and Thais are generally willing to discuss problems concerning their work with a supervisor once the boss has shown a willingness to support the employee in solving these problems. Whether they also feel free to discuss personal problems depends generally on the type of rapport they establish with their boss. Though many Thais (especially men) seem disinclined to bring up personal problems with their supervisors, others would deeply appreciate the chance to discuss such matters if only they had an understanding chief. The ideal supervisor, as mentioned earlier, is almost like a member of the family—an elder brother, respected relative, or particularly in this case a phîi liáng (often rendered in English as "nursemaid" or "trainer," though the literal meaning, "elder who looks after," better conveys the idea here). But speaking with sober Thai realism, one woman commented that most supervisors weren't ideal and thus one could generally not bring up personal matters. Another Thai pointed out that in a small, informal company one can more readily form a trusting relationship with the boss, thus leading the way to discussion of personal, as well as professional, problems.

One Thai with considerable supervisory experience stressed the importance of developing a technique or method of establishing trust so that an employee will confide without having the feeling the supervisor is invading his or her privacy. This might involve taking the subordinate out to lunch or at least away from the office and then gradually easing into a discussion of the problem rather than probing directly to the heart of the matter. Several Thais mentioned that as supervisors they would bring up a subordinate's personal problem only if it affected the staffer's work, though one also added that it would be hard to imagine a personal problem that didn't somehow impinge on one's work.

The importance of merely being a good listener should not be overlooked, and one young business administration graduate felt that though the supervisor should lend a receptive ear and offer suggestions, the boss should not actually make a decision for the subordinate. It was his impression that at least some Americans are not willing for one reason or another to serve as such a sounding board but might say something like, "Don't tell me; I've got enough problems already."

One thoughtful supervisor said that if the problem was clearly a technical one, she would send the subordinate to a training program of some kind, if only for half a day, so that the employee could pick up some needed skills. Her underlying philosophy could serve as a constructive reminder to all supervisors, for in speaking of how to handle an employee with technical deficiencies she said simply, "Train him, don't blame him."

One Thai suggested following a three-step process: first, simply talk the matter over with the subordinate; second, if performance still fails to improve, give a somewhat stronger warning; third, let the employee go. Americans sometimes go right to stage two and thus might catch a Thai subordinate more off guard than desirable. Another Thai stressed the importance of allowing the employee to tell his or her side of the story first; the supervisor can then point out in a sincere, reasoned manner some of the flaws which have been detected and suggest how the worker might set out to correct them.

Several Thais, again illustrating acute contextual sensitivity, emphasized the importance of flexibility, of handling each case in accord with all the surrounding variables rather than following any particularly set format. For instance, at times it may be best for the supervisor to talk to the subordinate directly; at other times it may be wiser to have a third person speak to the subordinate; in still other cases, it may be better to have the staffer submit a report first. This variation of approach is necessary to account for differing levels of education and different individual characteristics, preferences, or habits—lumped in Thai under the umbrella word *nísǎi*. Of utmost importance is that, whatever the approach, the problem should be handled *privately*—out of earshot and eyesight of others. Thais are particularly sensitive to public reprimand and generally experience a far greater degree of shame or loss of face in this context than do most Americans.

The Thai concern with being publicly embarrassed (*aaj*) and the extremes to which Thais will sometimes go to avoid it reveal an almost painful sensitivity when contrasted with American outspokenness. An American anthropologist, for example, once interviewed two village women whose husbands had taken second wives. Though deeply disturbed by their husbands' actions, they never once brought the matter up with their husbands, explaining that they were too aaj to do so. This sense of aaj-ness is also seen in the election of village headmen, for often there will be only one candidate. If there were rivals, the eventual winner would be embarrassed since the presence of competition would suggest doubt about his competence. The losing candidates would be embarrassed by the very fact that they lost. All of this can be easily avoided if only one candidate is presented, voted on, and elected.

American supervisors working with Thais should keep this concern for embarrassment in mind when speaking in even a mildly critical way by American standards. This is particularly true for new Thai employees who are not familiar with the more blunt, direct American approach. To give even mild correction, particularly if done publicly, can have a devastating effect, for example, on a new secretary and cause her "heart to disappear" (*cai hǎi*) in fear and embarrassment.

Some Americans, cognizant of this sensitivity, may go to the opposite extreme and be reluctant to tell Thais they are dissatisfied with their work. Though based on good intentions, this can have an equally negative impact, for a Thai may then work for many months thinking that his or her performance is satisfactory, only to learn one day that actually the boss is not happy. The American may in fact blow up, having bottled up dissatisfaction for too long; the Thai then ruefully thinks, "If only I had been told long ago, I could have easily done what was wanted."

The supervisor's position is clearly not an enviable one since one must walk an exceedingly narrow tightrope between bluntness and respect, candid criticism and cultural sensitivity. The best approach can be easily summarized: speak frankly but politely— and not in front of others. Unfortunately, it may not always be so easy to put into effect.

Appraisal and Promotion

Traditional Thai promotion practices reflect the deeply in- grained pattern of benevolent paternalism in which the *nai* ("master" but now usually rendered as "boss") rewarded *lûuk náwng* (subordi- nates) for respectful, obedient behavior. Though in theory a nai is a person of wrath as well as mercy, carrying the whip in one hand and the bag of money in the other, in practice the boss has been much freer in using the money rather than the whip. Generations of Thai subordinates have had coins dropped into their pockets far more than they have had the lash applied to their backs. In both government and business the immediate supervisor or department head shows considerable discretion in meting out promotions, and usually traits such as diligence, deference, and respect are accorded more importance than an objective analysis of the worker's performance and output. Though punishment is possible, it is the rare worker indeed, particularly in the bureaucracy, who is actually let go. Thais themselves say that they are too *cai aùn* (softhearted) to take such drastic measures.

Since promotion, particularly in government, is considered virtually certain, withholding the promotion is seen as a form of punishment. To insure that this does not occur, workers try to cultivate a good relationship with their immediate supervisors. In this situation there is a natural temptation to fawn and flatter, to "lick the shins" of a susceptible chief, notwithstanding the negative way in which society views such conduct. A Thai executive explains it this way: "In the U.S., work is a vehicle of recognition. Both Thais and Americans appreciate recognition. Americans know that one of the best ways to get recognition is through work. In Thailand you get recognition by being a best friend. If an employee pleases the boss and the boss likes the employee, the employee will get a good recommendation and a high job evaluation rating even though the work output was not outstanding."

Some up-and-coming young Thais who are familiar with Western recognition of hard work bridle at the traditional Thai system. A young Thai computer programmer educated in the West worked long and hard on a major project in a traditional Thai organization, thinking that his work would bring him a promotion. "I was really disappointed when my supervisor told me that I wouldn't get a promotion this year because I had gotten one last year. He said it was someone else's turn. Next year I won't bother trying so hard," he said.

The American pattern of promotion is based, at least in theory, on an objective appraisal of the worker's performance, so that the employee tries to earn a promotion by showing the supervisor that he or she is a competent, hardworking employee. Implicit in the American approach is the fragmentation of the personality that we mentioned in discussing friendship, the tendency to view the individual as a composite of distinct achievements and interests; for the supervisor, in making an objective assessment, is (again theoretically) evaluating the achievements and output of the worker rather than personal behavior. It is the employee's performance rather than the individual that is being scrutinized to determine whether he or she has earned the promotion. In fact if the assessment is to be truly objective, the supervisor will consciously try to avoid bringing personal considerations to bear on the decision, viewing such subjective criteria as irrelevant and unfair to the worker involved.

This objective, somewhat impersonal approach clearly clashes with the highly personalized manner in which promotion has traditionally been handled in Thailand. Rather than earning a promotion based on performance, the Thai subordinate has literally "slid his position (up)" (*dâi lŷ̂an tamnaèng*) through deference and obedience to his superior. Though the merit system of promotion has been introduced into Thailand, its actual implementation is probably fairly well limited to large, modern firms. As for smaller, more traditional companies and the massive bureaucracy, the situation appears to be in considerable flux. As one Thai summed it up: "We now have everything—the merit system, the patronage system, and no system."

Implementation of the more objective merit system runs smack into a host of deep-seated traditions. In substituting objective criteria for broad supervisory discretion, the paternalistic superior/subordinate relationship is undermined and the personal bond between the two weakened by the intrusion of an unfamiliar piece of paper—the standardized rating form. In fact the whole notion of objective assessment, embodying as it does negative as well as positive comments, does not fit easily into a society where such a premium is placed on avoidance of the unpleasant and on acute sensitivity to psychic comfort. For how can one *kreng cai* (take the other person's feelings into account) and avoid making the other individual feel *aaj* (embarrassed) when one is telling an employee he or she is doing a rotten job? Americans are accustomed to making a sharp distinction between the individual's achievements and the individual her- or himself (per se). Thais—at least those influenced by Western management procedures—tend to view the standardized rating form as a well-sharpened knife which might better be left in its scabbard.

Many large American companies have a standardized evaluation process which assumes that a small percentage of workers will fall into the "high achievers" category, the majority will fall into the "average" category, and a third group will fall into the "unacceptable" category. One American executive recalls trying to implement this system in Thailand. "At first I couldn't get the Thai supervisors to identify the high and low performers. Everyone knew who the top performers were, but no one wanted to be forced to identify them because, in so doing, they would also have to identify the poor performers and face the tough questions of early retirement or termination. By moving everyone into the middle they felt more comfortable."

Further inhibiting critical appraisal, let alone dismissal, is the more personalized approach traditionally taken to hiring someone in the first place. Often an influential person would *fàak* (entrust in the sense of sending or handing over) someone to an employer that he knew, thus making it difficult for the employer to fire the worker without straining the relationship with the sender. The prospective employee might secure a *còdmǎaj nǎeam tua* from the benefactor, which literally means a "letter for introducing oneself." Though this is now often translated into English as a letter of recommendation, it is clearly not the frank, critical appraisal of the candidate's qualifications that the English term implies. Rather it is more of a lubricating device to smooth the entry of the candidate into the employer's office—a message from the sender to the employer saying in effect: "This is the person I am sending to work for you."

Thais who have studied and mastered the more objective, impersonal management techniques of the West find themselves in an anomalous position when they return home. Ready tô apply their new learning, they often discover that the entrenched system is not particularly receptive to their rigorous, modern approach.

To such individuals, American, European, or Westernized-Thai firms, despite their more demanding pace and greater insecurity, appear to offer more rewards than would be forthcoming from a less dynamic but more sabaaj government sinecure. With a private firm, if they do something prominent or outstanding, it will be rewarded, whereas such performance in the government might go unnoticed unless they play up to their boss.

Thais have throughout their history successfully integrated various aspects of other cultures into their own way of life. This capacity for careful assimilation will be severely tested as attempts are made to adopt Western management styles when one considers the appreciable gap between benevolent paternalism and management by objective, between interpersonal sensitivity and impersonal ratings. But given the strength and resiliency of the traditional culture and the long-standing Thai capacity for adjustment and adaptation, the twain just might somehow meet.

Decision Making

Contrasting American and Thai views toward authority, hierarchy, time, and confrontation manifest themselves in differing procedures of decision making in the two societies. The American notion that authority is to be challenged and power fragmented leads to a more participatory, as opposed to authoritarian, approach, which is reinforced by the ideal of egalitarianism in which each person is deemed to have an opinion worth taking into account. Decision making in many instances is thus a group process, which makes extensive use of committees and conferences.

The traditional Thai pattern has been more authoritarian or autocratic, and although these terms have a negative connotation in the American context, they clearly fit well with the strong vertical orientation of Thai society and the belief that a leader derives power at least in part from past moral excellence. The leader then is the logical one to have the authority to make decisions and bear the responsibility for their consequences. If a supervisor does call a meeting, it is often to issue orders or to have subordinates substantiate the supervisor's predetermined point of view, decisions, or policies. Even if a majority of the subordinates are in disagreement, the boss's point of view will generally carry the day—reminiscent of Lincoln's cabinet meeting in which all voted no except the President, who then said that the ayes had it.

One perceptive Thai who has had considerable experience with Thai and American businesspeople felt that the different approach to decision making is occasioned more by the cultural values and corresponding managerial systems of the two societies than by a difference in personality of the leaders themselves. He felt that both Thai and American leaders tend to be authoritarian but that the participatory American system, rooted in egalitarianism and distrust of power, forces the American executives to listen to their subordinates. No cultural constraint of this kind generally operates on Thai leaders.

This is not to say that Americans are never authoritarian. Commenting on American academics she knows, one Thai university staffer said that, in her experience, when Americans who are knowledgeable in a field think they are right, they are not much interested in consulting other experts. Or if they do, they don't pay particular heed to the advice if it clashes with their point of view. In the academic setting, where the system does not force participation to the same extent as in the corporate boardroom, the American decision maker is freer to display authoritarian colors.

Foreign observers and even Westernized Thais themselves often speak critically of the unwillingness of Thai subordinates at every level to take responsibility. Rather, they will push responsibility up into the hands of their superiors, who will in turn pass the buck still higher until it reaches the ultimate position, thereby burdening top levels with minor decisions.

If one considers the subjective view of the subordinates, however, it might be somewhat unfair to look at their conduct as a shirking or abdication of responsibility. In traditional hierarchical terms it was literally not their place to make decisions. Higher-ranking officials, generally older and more experienced, were entrusted with these matters; for a subordinate to presume to exercise such authority would be a clear case of overstepping one's station. The Thai propensity for looking to the leader is reflected in such proverbs as these: "The phûûjàj (literally "big person," adult, chief) has already bathed in the hot water" (compare the English saying, "He's been through the mill," or "He knows the ropes") and "Follow the phûûjàj, and the dog won't bite," which clearly indicates that one should look to the leader, to the person with rank and experience, to tackle the complexities of decision making. The seriousness of such an undertaking is reflected in the Thai word for "decide" (tàtsǐncai), which literally means "the mind passes sentence."

We mentioned earlier that one of the results of the Americans' relationship to their natural environment (i.e., their attempt to control or master it) is an emphasis on measurability and statistical data. This is clearly reflected in American decision making, where leaders want to get the "hard facts," systematize them, and project them into the future. Thais traditionally have not relied so heavily on concrete facts in arriving at decisions, and Thai administrators are not as convinced as Americans that their own actions can influence a given outcome. Thais accept the fact that superhuman forces are at work which make it difficult to draw a direct correlation between the administrator's alternatives and various resulting outcomes.

One of the superhuman forces is the Buddhist concept of karma, the accumulated merit and demerit from past lives and their influence on the present one; another is chance or luck, which suggests the occurrence of events which are for the most part beyond one's control. Karma and luck affect not only the success of the administrator's own actions but also the success of others upon whom the administrator must depend for support. As James Mosel explained it,

> Thus he must evaluate the merit and luck of others and take this into account in making choices. For this reason, the Thai administrator gives greater weight to personal and particularistic criteria in figuring consequences than does his Western counterpart. His evaluations appear to be more people-oriented than program-oriented.

Americans' stress on statistical data tends to make their decision making systematic while their concept of time plays a part in making it decisive. In productively organizing future time, Americans often set deadlines for making a decision. Time marches on and one must keep in step with it. Thus, says the American, "I'll give myself until next Wednesday to make a decision on this matter so that we can then move forward on other things." The American may well recognize that the surrounding circumstances are not clear, that there is "a lot of gray here"; but the fast approaching deadline forces the issue into black and white and demands a prompt decision in favor of one or the other. To do otherwise would be vacillating and indecisive.

Since they don't share Americans' lineal notion of time and the corresponding sense of urgency, Thais have not felt it necessary to pressure themselves into what they might view as hurried or impulsive decisions. This attitude has been reinforced by the belief in karma and luck, which clearly do not fit readily into a next-Wednesday deadline. Traditional Thai administrators may thus postpone decisions until there is some indication that luck is with them; or they may feel that there is no need to make a decision at all and simply allow events to work themselves out in accord with the superhuman forces behind them. In the latter case the Thais merely look to nature to take its course, or in Thai, *taam bun taam kam* (leave it to merit and karma).

Thais appear to be somewhat ambivalent concerning American decision-making techniques. On the one hand, they tend to view the systematic, facts-oriented American method as modern and efficient, and they generally admire decisiveness, so in this regard they look favorably on the American approach to decision making. In fact one of the major Thai complaints with some recent civilian governments has been that they were not decisive enough. Since these civilian leaders were trying to allow for more democratic participation in government and were consciously allowing different factions to be heard, they naturally often had to delay making decisions until various viewpoints were considered. But the Thai (or at least Bangkokian) citizenry, accustomed to the decisive authority of the monarch and subsequent military rulers, looked on the accommodating civilian leaders as weak and ineffective.

On the other hand, Thais feel that the systematic, decisive American approach to decision making often does not satisfactorily take into account intangible or subtle factors, such as opinions and ideas which cannot be articulated in open discussion, personal sensitivities, and a sense of timing. If something cannot be graphed, charted, or voiced, Americans tend to pay it no heed; in so doing—from the Thai perspective, at least—they are missing sizable portions of the overall decision-making picture. Thais want ultimately to be decisive, but, at the same time, they want all factors to be taken into account. Since their approach may consume considerable time, Americans may view it as cumbersome.

As for the actual conduct of the discussions leading up to the decision, our earlier comments concerning emotional expression and confrontation apply in this forum as well. The more frank, direct, often argumentative American approach contrasts with the less assertive, indirect Thai pattern. In fact one difficulty that American Peace Corps volunteers have had in working smoothly in the Thai bureaucracy is that, in the words of one Thai, they sometimes don't know *wíthii phûud* (the way to speak). Thus, if they attempt to put forward their point in an overly blunt, abrasive fashion, they will alienate more than assist, even though they may be admired for their idealism and the substance of some of their ideas. Content will go unnoticed if presented in an inappropriate form. Wíthii phûud embodies all of the ingredients of smooth interpersonal relationships (*kreng cai*—surface harmony, tact, politeness, avoidance of negative, hostile comments, etc.) discussed earlier.

At least some Thais see problems which their acute sensitivity presents in effectively discussing debatable points. Whereas Americans try (although obviously not always successfully) to divorce their personal feelings toward others in the debate from the content of the ideas they are expressing, Thais find it more difficult to make such a distinction. Opposition to one's opinions is taken personally, and Thais generally cannot engage in an intellectual argument without becoming emotionally affected. To prevent this clash, Thais may hold back rather than come to grips with the question at hand if it involves a difference of opinion. Surface harmony will be preserved, but the problem will be left unresolved.

The assertive, content-centered American pattern of decision making culminates in the desire for a clear-cut, specific outcome so that everyone involved will know exactly what the decision is and what must be done to further its implementation. Since the Thai approach has tended to mute, rather than emphasize, differences, the decision may be correspondingly less precise or, in some instances, actually ambiguous. A certain measure of specificity is sacrificed so that no feelings will be severely bruised. This approach also ensures a flexibility which will take into account intangible and superhuman factors as well as the facts.

This lack of precision and acceptance of ambiguity is most noticeable at village-level meetings, where a topic may be brought up, discussed, and then dropped without any clear-cut resolution. At one such meeting, for example, the question was raised as to whether some old members of the village school committee would retire. One committee member, formerly village headman, said that he would like to leave the committee but was urged to stay on by other members. He explicitly stated several times that he wanted to retire, but each time he was asked to stay. Eventually, the meeting disbanded with no indication as to whether he would stay or retire.

From an American perspective such uncertainty is troublesome;

too much is left up in the air. Did he or didn't he retire? Let's get this straight. The villagers, however, were apparently unconcerned about this ambiguity, if indeed they even perceived the outcome as ambiguous. For it was precisely the uncertainty, the things left up in the air, that would enable the matter to be resolved in a way that would be acceptable to those concerned. The former headman could go home, discuss the matter with his family, and eventually decide on the best course of action. Here, in the privacy of his home, he would have the chance to talk over certain covert or intangible factors that could not be comfortably aired in a public meeting; for instance, was the new headman trying to force him off the committee, did the other committee members really want him to stay or were they just being publicly polite, and what would happen if he should accept their expressed show of support and decide to stay on? Things will eventually work their way out—the former headman will either retire or he'll stay on—without the necessity of a clear-cut, possibly embarrassing public decision.

The traditional Thai pattern of decision making, with its autocratic and at times ambiguous overtones, does not typify certain modern, progressive Bangkok firms which, like their Western counterparts, strive for participation and precision. In between these few large-scale enterprises and the traditionally run small businesses lie some middle-to-large-sized companies which feature what might be called a "mixed system," that is, long-standing authoritarian decision making merged with modern management practices. Thus, the chief still wields considerable power but also delegates authority and responsibility more than in the past. One Thai professor who has served as a consultant to several companies of this type said that there are often two kinds of meetings: the traditional meeting to hand out orders and the modern meeting which features a group approach to decision making.

Planning

The Americans' notion of planning springs naturally from their lineal concept of time, their belief that one is in control of the environment, and their positive view of human-initiated change. The ribbon of time is chopped into segments; each segment is planned, and future events are fit into a schedule. Though obviously contributing to smooth organization and efficiency, detailed planning has a built-in rigidity. Once the time has been scheduled, there is a tendency to use it as designated, even though it may not be necessary or advantageous to do so. If Americans have allocated a given amount of time to a certain activity, they may be able to change it once or twice, but they cannot continually move the walls of their time compartments back and forth—even though in some instances such flexibility would be desirable. Thais sometimes use the word *rádkum* (to be airtight, without any loopholes) to describe American planning and juxtapose it with the less efficient but more flexible Thai way, in which for every rule, there is an exception.

The more cyclical Thai concept of time combined with the traditional disinclination to initiate change (all things, remember, are constantly changing by themselves) have tended to preclude a compartmentalized organization of future time for productive use. When the unforeseeable, superhuman forces of karma, chance, and luck are added to this, it is clear why Thais have traditionally placed more store in Buddhist chants, spirit offerings, and astrological divination than in rigorous, long-range planning and rigid scheduling of future time.

The sequential, linear American approach to planning is seen as underlying management development programs. If manager A works in department X for six months, then takes Y training program, and then spends two years on the road, he will be ready in three years to take over manager B's job. This type of long-range, linear programming is essentially alien to the traditional Thai way of thinking, in which things have generally been allowed to resolve themselves over a period of time. Preparation might be made, that is, a son or daughter might be generally educated to take over part of a business, but the young person's training and development would not be predetermined to the same extent as they would for an American manager.

At the more mundane level, Thais generally (particularly in the rural areas) do not share the American penchant for keeping lists of things to do and preparing family budgets. As one Thai (again manifesting extreme realism) expressed it, "We don't like to think about things far into the future; we equate it with just dreaming. Why bother?" Two Thais interviewed for this study used exactly the same sentence to describe the traditional Thai disinclination to plan ahead: "*Khon thai wang paěn maî khỏy pen*" (freely translated as, "Thais are just not good at making plans"). This would be particularly true for long-range plans, and the Thais irreverently refer to that epitome of comprehensiveness, the "master plan," as a *paen mâe* or "mother's plan." (*Maê*, the Thai word for "mother," is pronounced exactly the same way as the "ma" in "master"; thus the play on words to get "mother's plan.")

The vertical organizational structure discussed earlier, in which each department or unit is pretty much an entity unto itself, does not make planning in Thailand any easier. Thus, centralized planning, embodying as it does a horizontal coordination, is simply unfeasible in the face of strong structural constraints against cross-departmental interaction.

As in many other areas, it is again necessary to distinguish the planning methods of a few sophisticated Bangkok companies, the government bureaucracy, and the large number of small, often family-run businesses. Operations of many of the large, modern firms are well planned in both the short- and long-range. The Royal Thai government develops a comprehensive five-year plan for the country periodically. Though long-range planning has been introduced, it has often been difficult to actually put the plans into effect because many high-level officials are well educated in a specific technical field but have little training in management techniques. Since they are not well versed in the art of making plans, they often are not entirely comfortable in planning. There has been, however, an increase in government officials with advanced training in public administration.

An American professor who studied administrative practices in the Thai bureaucracy concluded that Thai administrators may substitute for planning a strategy of what might be called coping, in which they will plan for a very short time span, so short that it would hardly qualify as planning in the American sense. Coping involves considerable trial and error, as the administrator endeavors to remain loose and uncommitted and thus free to take advantage of circumstances as they present themselves. Though Thai administrators have become highly adept at the art of coping, their methods have not been embodied in an overt doctrine with formal rules and precepts as has been the case with American planning.

As for the small businesses, traditionally there has been no formal planning at all. This is not to say that they don't have objectives, for at the very least they will be in business for some purpose—to maximize profit, to establish a good reputation, to contribute to society, etc. But this objective may not be written down or stated explicitly; it may exist solely in the top person's mind. Even those companies which have something they call a plan may really simply have a statement of policy rather than a full-fledged plan with forecasts, objectives, strategies, and tactics. Like the administrator, the flexible small businessperson copes and is ready to shift and weave to meet the demands of the everchanging market. No restrictive long-range plans for this adaptable, pragmatic, independent soul; if the small businessperson plans at all, it will be, in the felicitous words of one Thai, "*ngâi ngâi sân sân*"—very easy, very short.

Negotiation

The negotiating techniques which characterize the two societies neatly parallel their respective approaches to decision making and planning, which, as we have just seen, are rooted deeply in cultural values. The precision, directness and productive use of time which characterize American decision making and planning are again evident in negotiating practices. Also apparent is the compartmentalization of business and social life, for in the negotiating forum, it's "let's get down to business" and save the drinks and camaraderie until later. A negotiating strategy is carefully mapped out well in advance, the opposing side's position is scrutinized, and a series of proposals, counterproposals, fallback positions, and concessions is thoroughly rehearsed. Great emphasis is placed on being able to support a particular position with a persuasive set of statistics or facts. Like a knight about to enter a joust, the American negotiator wants to be certain that there are no obvious chinks in the verbal armor which might render him or her vulnerable to a well-placed thrust from the opposition.

From the Thai perspective, the American preoccupation with persuasive speech, supporting facts, and quick arrival at the main issue causes them to overlook intangible, covert factors (just as in decision making), such as human relationships, customs, and timing. While Thais appreciate the systematic efficiency of the American approach and view it as businesslike and professional, they at the same time feel it lacks something in the way of flexibility and congeniality.

Thai negotiations are more like a leisurely game of badminton than a dead-serious joust, and conviviality, sympathy, and patience take precedence over earnest, hardheaded bargaining. Since Thais do not feel pressured to quickly and persuasively present their position, they begin negotiation not with a highly specific strategy but with a broad, general objective.

Of primary importance is the establishment of a good personal relationship based on trust and understanding. Rather than getting right down to business, the two parties will often have drinks or lunch together, search out their common interests, and perhaps meet later to share a favorite pastime. As the social relationship develops, business will be blended in; and eventually the specific point being negotiated, say the price of goods, will be resolved. But the agreement will not so much be hammered into shape as patted into place, slowly and gently. No need for a clear-cut, immediate resolution. Just give things enough time, and eventually everything will work out. Generally, there will first be some type of broad, informal agreement. The exact details and a more formal embodiment of their understanding will come later.

Often direct appeals to sympathy are involved, and the final agreement may reflect the desire to help a friend more than the wish to gain an advantage. One side may agree to an arrangement in which it receives no benefit simply as a personal favor to the other party. For example, a seller may approach a buyer and tell him that he desperately needs some money this month to help his family. Even though the buyer does not need any more of the seller's product, he may agree to buy and stock it just because he wants to help the seller who, right now, has a pressing cash problem. Though this may appear not to be "good business," Thais might say that all cannot be measured in the profit-and-loss statement.

This leniency in helping someone in trouble should not be confused, however, with a wide-eyed naivete, for, as mentioned earlier, the Thais have long been known for their keen diplomatic skill, and they waste little sympathy on one who is easily duped. Perhaps the key to their success in international as well as smaller-scale negotiations could be summarized in one word: patience. Rather than hurriedly agreeing to something they might later regret, they adopt a "let's wait and see" attitude. While they are waiting and seeing, things have a way of working themselves out. Both sides are somehow satisfied, and relations are kept on a smooth, even keel. As one professor aptly phrased it, "We are more cool in Thailand, for we always know that we have enough time."

8

Learning from One Another

We have been busily fitting different pieces of information into our Thai and American cultural mosaic. Let's now step back for a moment and take a look at the overall design which is emerging. Similarities are definitely there, for both people are freedom-loving, independent, practical, down-to-earth, individualistic, and self-reliant. Both quickly turn away from arrogance, stuffiness, and pomposity. There is, then, a strong common core of values, which both peoples can build on as they sort out the whys and wherefores of some of their differences.

Though these dissimilarities appear numerous, many are related to one another; and so what seems to be a wide variety of almost miscellaneous cultural contrasts and differences narrows down to a few key ones which spiral out and manifest themselves in various aspects of life. In fact, there are two broad, basic differences which subsume nearly all those covered in this book: (1) different attitudes toward time and the natural environment and (2) different social structures and concepts of authority. Getting a handle on these two fundamental differences will contribute more than anything else to furthering the cause of mutual understanding between Thais and Americans. The American values (lineal concept of time, control of natural environment, egalitarian social order, and distrust of power and authority) and their Thai opposites (cyclical time sense, accommodation to nature, hierarchy, and deference to authority) manifest themselves again and again in the social, business, educational, and political spheres of the two societies. These fundamental differences are the key to understanding how and why certain basic ideas are played out so differently in each of the two societies.

Take the case of democracy, an idea originating in the West, which features egalitarian participation, fragmentation of power, and challenge to authority. What happens when the concept is transferred to Thailand, where superior/subordinate relationships, respect for power, and deference to authority have traditionally held sway? Since the mentality of a people forged through the centuries is not going to magically change at the introduction of a new word, Thais are still struggling with ways to reconcile the Western notion of democracy with their long-standing concept of government as a strong, wise, but indulgent father. Rather than concerning themselves with the notion of the legislature as a forum where competing views are aired and compromise forged, Thai villagers have tended to zero in on their personal relationship with their representatives, treating them as the traditional influential patrons who could be depended on for protection and assistance. A new political ideology has been introduced, but it has been interpreted in terms of traditional values.

The desire for a uniquely Thai democracy was expressed in 1966 by the ruling regime in these colorful words:

> Let us hope that our democracy is like a plant having roots in Thai soil. It should grow amidst the beating sun and whipping rain. It should produce bananas, mangoes, rambutans, mangosteens, and durians; and not apples, grapes, dates, plums, or horse chestnuts.

The difficulties involved in introducing alien ideas are apparent in the business sector as well, where Western management practices often do not graft easily onto the traditional autocratic organizational structure. One large Thai enterprise, for example, had a clear three-tier management system patterned after the

Western model. But *all* outgoing correspondence was still being passed to the chief executive for checking before being sent. A new system had supposedly been installed, but the underlying behavioral pattern—the need for the top man to know and be responsible for all—was untouched by the innovation.

Thais, then, are trying to select those Western ideas, procedures, and systems which will assist them in their economic development and improve the material quality of their life, but which will also allow them to maintain their cultural integrity. Thais and Americans who possess both the up-to-date technical expertise and Western management techniques, as well as the sensitivity to know when and how to adapt and apply them, are a valuable resource in this transitional period.

As in so many areas of life, it is the little, almost unnoticed things which can make all the difference in Thai attitudes toward Americans working in Thailand. So much depends on whether an American manager, for example, is perceived as treating Thai colleagues with respect (*kiàd*). Perhaps something the American says or, equally important, the *way* it is said might be construed as patronizing or even insulting, as if the American is talking down to his or her other coworkers, implying that they do not know as much as the manager. Thais want to feel that they are equal partners, not second-class citizens, in the American company for which they work, and they are supersensitive to any signs that they are being treated more like the latter than the former.

If, on the other hand, an American does treat a Thai colleague with kiàd, the Thai will be intensely loyal and probably won't leave the company even though the pay and working conditions might be better elsewhere. This willingness to stay would not be so much because of loyalty to the company itself, but because of the personal relationship which had been formed with American coworkers or a supervisor.

Given the prominent position of the United States on the world scene and the long-standing desire of Thailand to borrow certain aspects of Western culture, the assimilation process has tended to move in one direction. This is too bad. For despite the material comforts and modern conveniences which the United States provides, many Americans seem to be continually looking for inner peace that has somehow eluded them. Thais have something to offer here. As a former Thai ambassador to the U.S. once told an American audience, "We turn to you for technical help, but not in the search of happiness. We would like to teach you the art of being happy."

The Thais have mastered this art because long ago they learned the secret of living comfortably with their environment and with one another. Interpersonal relationships, characterized by a constant respect for the dignity and psychological integrity of the other person, reveal a wisdom somehow lacking in the American propensity to look out for number one. One social scientist has termed Thai politeness one of the most civilized modes of social interaction, for it is based on a fundamental concern with behaving so as to least disturb others and thus permit them to act in socially easy, uncomplicated ways.

Even a superficial understanding of this smooth, sensitive mode of interaction would be worth more than a bookshelf of the latest pop psychology manuals, for Thais don't need a book to tell them that "I'm OK, you're OK." Nor do Thais need to be formally trained in sensitivity, for their whole way of life has been a centuries-long sensitivity training par excellence.

Thais could thus help Americans to make their lives more inwardly comfortable, just as Americans could help Thais to make theirs more outwardly comfortable. Each has a gap that could at least partially be filled by drawing on the strengths of the other. Thus, the cultures complement each other, and Americans and Thais, working together as partners, can help one another pick and choose the ingredients which will improve the quality of life of both countries.

Bibliography

Amrand, Pimsai. *My Family, My Friends, and I*. Bangkok: United Production, 1977.

Anderson, Dole A. *Marketing and Development: The Thailand Experience*. East Lansing, MI: Michigan State University Press, 1970.

Ayal, E.B. "Value Systems and Economic Development in Japan and Thailand." *Journal of Social Issues* 19 (1963): 35.

Barry, J. *Thai Students in the U.S.: A Study in Attitude Change*. Cornell University Data Paper Number 66. Ithaca, NY: Cornell University, 1967.

Benedict, Ruth. *Thai Culture and Behavior*. Cornell University Data Paper Number 4. Ithaca, NY: Cornell University, 1943.

Bilmes, Jack. *Misinformation and Ambiguity in Verbal Interaction: A Northern Thai Example*. Paper presented at American Anthropological Association Meeting at New Orleans, November 1973 (Photocopied).

Blanchard, Wendell. *Thailand: Its People, Its Society, Its Culture*. New Haven, CT: Human Relations Area Files, 1958.

Bunnag, Jane. "Loose Structure: Fact or Fancy? Thai Society Reexamined." *The Journal of the Siam Society* 59 (January 1971): 1-23.

114

Busch, Noel F. *Thailand: An Introduction to Modern Siam.* Princeton,NJ: Van Nostrand, 1959.

Chu, Valentin. *Thailand Today: A Visit to Modern Siam.* New York: Crowell, 1968.

Condon, John, and F. Yousef. *An Introduction to Intercultural Communication.* Indianapolis and New York: Bobbs-Merrill, 1975.

Cooke, Joseph R. *Pronominal Reference in Thai, Burmese, and Vietnamese.* Berkeley and Los Angeles: University of California Publications in Linguistics Number 52, 1968.

Cooper, Robert and Nanthapa. *Culture Shock Thailand.* Singapore: Times Books International, 1984.

de Tocqueville, Alexis. *Democracy in America.* New York: Harper and Row, 1966.

Deyo, Frederic C. *Organization and Its Socio-Cultural Setting: A Case Study of Structural Compensation in an Atomistic Society.* University of Singapore Sociology Working Paper Number 41, 1975.

———. *Decision Making and Supervisory Authority in Cross-Cultural Perspective.* University of Singapore Sociology Working Paper Number 55, 1976.

Dhani, Prince. "The Old Siamese Conception of the Monarchy." *The Journal of the Siam Society* 36 (December 1947): 91-106.

Embree, John F. "Thailand—A Loosely Structured Social System." *American Anthropologist* 52 (1950): 181.

Enright, D.J. "Thai Personalities." *Encounter* 32 (1969): 27.

Evers, Hans-Dieter, ed. *Loosely Structured Social Systems: Thailand in Comparative Perspective.* Yale University Cultural Report Series Number 17, New Haven, CT: Yale University, 1969.

Fieg, John P. *The Thai Way: A Study of Cultural Values.* Washington, DC: Meridian House International, 1976.

———, and C. Lenore Yaffee. *Adjusting to the U.S.A.—Orientation for International Students.* Washington, DC: Meridian House International, 1977.

Foreign Areas Studies Division. *U.S. Army Area Handbook for Thailand.* Washington, DC: The American University, 1963.

Foster, Brian L. "Friendship in Rural Thailand." *Ethnology* 15 (1976): 251-67.

Gardiner, H. "Expression of Anger Among Thais—Some Preliminary Findings." *Psychologia* 11 (1968): 221.

Haas, Mary R. *Thai-English Student's Dictionary.* Stanford, CA: Stanford University Press, 1964.

Hall, Edward T. *The Silent Language.* Greenwich, CT: Fawcett, 1959.

Hanks, L.M. "The Corporation and the Entourage: A Comparison of Thai and American Social Organization." *Catalyst 2* (1966): 55-63.

———. "Merit and Power in the Thai Social Order." *American Anthropologist* 64 (1962): 1247.

Heine-Geldern. *Conceptions of State and Kingship in Southeast Asia,* Cornell University Data Paper Number 18. Ithaca, NY: Cornell University, 1956.

Ingersoll, Jasper. "Fatalism in Rural Thailand." *Anthropological Quarterly* 39 (1966): 205.

Kerdsawang, B.M. *Siam—The Land of Smiles.* Bangkok: Pramuan Sarn, n.d.

Klausner, William, and Kampan. *Conflict or Communication.* Bankok: Business Information and Research Co., Ltd., n.d.

Komin, Suntaree. *The Relationships between Emotions and Cultural Values.* Doctoral dissertation. Honolulu: University of Hawaii, 1975.

Le May, Reginald (trans.). *Siamese Tales Old and New.* London: Unwin Brothers, 1930.

Martyn-Johns, Tom. "Thailand's Tangled Tapestry." *Asian Business and Industry* (December 1977): 53-59.

Meng, Ho Wing. *Asian Values and Modernization—A Critical Interpretation.* University of Singapore Department of Philosophy Occasional Paper Number 1. Singapore: University of Singapore, 1976.

116

Mezey, M.L. "Functions of a Minimal Legislature—Role Perceptions of Thai Legislators." *Western Political Quarterly* 25 (1972): 686.

Moerman, Michael. *Western Culture and the Thai Way of Life.* Training handout. Washington, DC: Peace Corps, 1965.

Mortlock, Elizabeth. *At Home in Thailand.* Bangkok: United States Information Service, 1986.

———. *Welcoming a Thai.* Bankok: United States Information Service, 1986.

Mosel, James N. "Fatalism in Thai Bureaucratic Decision-Making." *Anthropological Quarterly* 39 (1966): 191.

———. "Thai Administrative Behavior." In *Toward the Comparative Study of Public Administration,* edited by W. Siffing. Bloomington, IN: Indiana University Press, 1957.

Nakamura, Hajime. *Ways of Thinking of Eastern Peoples: India-China-Tibet-Japan.* Honolulu: East-West Center, 1964.

Nakata, Thinpan. "Political Legitimacy in Thailand: Problems and Prospects." *Journal of Social Science Review* 1 (March 1976): 42-121.

Negandhi, Anant R. *Organization Theory in an Open System.* New York: Dunellen, 1975.

Numnonda, Thamsook. "The First American Advisers in Thai History." *The Journal of the Siam Society* 62 (July 1974): 121-48.

Pendleton, Robert L. *Thailand: Aspects of Landscape and Life.* New York: Duell, Sloan, and Pearce, 1962.

Phillips, Herbert P. *Thai Attitudes toward the American Presence.* Special Paper Number 2, Center for South and Southeast Asia Studies, Berkeley: University of California, 1971.

———. *Thai Peasant Personality.* Berkeley and Los Angeles: University of California, 1966.

Phitakspraiwan, Titima. "The Acceptance of Western Culture in Thailand." *East Asian Cultural Studies* 6 (1967): 190-200.

Piker, Steven. "Friendship to the Death in Rural Thai Society." *Human Organization* 27 (1968): 200-04.

Pramoj, Kukrit. *Myang Maya*. Bangkok: Kawnaa Publisher,1965.
Presenting Thailand. Bangkok: Public Relations Department, Office of the Prime Minister, 1968.
Rabibhadana, Akin. *The Organization of Thai Society in the Early Bangkok Period*. Cornell University Data Paper Number 74. Ithaca, NY: Cornell University Press, 1969.
Redding, Gordon. "Bridging the Culture Gap." *Asian Business and Industry* (April 1978): 45-52.
―――. "National Traits." *Asian Business and Industry* (September 1977): 60-64.
Seely, Francis M. "Some Problems in Translating the Scriptures into Thai" *The Bible Translator* 8 (April 1957): 49-61.
Sithi-Amnuai. "The Asian Mind." *Asia* 11 (1968): 78-91.
Skinner, G. William, and A. Thomas Kirsch, eds. *Change and Persistence in Thai Society*. Ithaca, NY: Cornell University Press, 1975.
Smith, Ronald Bishop. *Siam or the History of the Thais from 1569 A.D. to 1824 A.D.* Bethesda, MD: Decatur Press, 1967.
Stewart, Edward C. *American Cultural Patterns: A Cross-Cultural Perspective*. Yarmouth, ME: Intercultural Press, 1972.
Sukwiwat, Mayoree. *Adjusting to Life Abroad*. (in Thai). Bangkok: United States Information Service, 1986.
―――. *Thai Hospitality* (in Thai). Bangkok: United States Information Service, 1986.
Suvanjata, Titya. "Is Thai Social System Loosely Structured?" *Journal of Social Science Review* 1 (March 1976): 171-88.
Thailand in Brief. Bangkok: Public Relations Department, Office of the Prime Minister, 1977.
Thailand Panorama. Bangkok: Public Relations Department, Office of the Prime Minister, 1972.
Wichiencharoen, Adul. "Social Values in Thailand." *Journal of Social Science Review* 1 (March 1976): 122-70.
Wood, W.A.R. *A History of Siam*. Bangkok: Siam Barnakich Press, 1926.

Yamklinfung, Prasert. "Family, Religion and Socio-Economic Change in Thailand." *East Asian Cultural Studies* 13 (March 1974): 20-31.

Zimmerman, Robert F. "Student 'Revolution' in Thailand: The End of the Thai Bureaucratic Polity?" *Asian Survey* 14 (June 1974): 509-29.